America's Beginnings

America's Beginnings

The Dramatic Events that Shaped a Nation's Character

Tony Williams

ROWMAN & LITTLEFIELD PUBLISHERS, INC.
Lanham • Boulder • New York • Toronto • Plymouth, UK

In association with
THE COLONIAL WILLIAMSBURG FOUNDATION
Williamsburg, Virginia
Colonial Williamsburg

ROWMAN & LITTLEFIELD PUBLISHERS, INC.

In association with THE COLONIAL WILLIAMSBURG FOUNDATION

Published in the United States of America
by Rowman & Littlefield Publishers, Inc.
A wholly owned subsidiary of The Rowman & Littlefield Publishing Group, Inc.
4501 Forbes Boulevard, Suite 200, Lanham, Maryland 20706
www.rowmanlittlefield.com

Estover Road, Plymouth PL6 7PY, United Kingdom

Distributed by National Book Network

British Library Cataloguing in Publication Information Available

Library of Congress Cataloging-in-Publication Data

Williams, Tony, 1970–
America's beginnings : the dramatic events that shaped a nation's character / Tony Williams.
    p. cm.
Includes bibliographical references and index.
ISBN 978-1-4422-0487-4 (cloth : alk. paper)
ISBN 978-1-4422-0489-8 (electronic)
    1. United States—History—Colonial period, ca. 1600–1775. I. Title.
E188.W615 2010
973.2—dc22   2010027630

∞ ™ The paper used in this publication meets the minimum requirements of American National Standard for Information Sciences—Permanence of Paper for Printed Library Materials, ANSI/NISO Z39.48-1992.

Printed in the United States of America

Contents

Preface and Acknowledgments

*T*he Lost Colony. Jamestown. The Pequot War. Bacon's Rebellion. The Salem Witch Trials. The Great Awakening. The Stamp Act. The Boston Tea Party. Bunker Hill. The Declaration of Rights. Valley Forge. The Newburgh Conspiracy. Shays' Rebellion. The *Federalist*.

Most Americans remember something about these events, or at least remember studying about them for some exam. But do we really understand the difference between Jamestown and Plymouth? Or between the Declaration of Rights and the Declaration of Independence? Do we really care about Roger Williams and Anne Hutchinson?

Recent interest in America's beginnings has been dubbed "Founder's Chic," as if the popular interest in our nation's origins were a passing fad. I believe it is more than that—and that it has to be more than that. Understanding America's beginnings is key to understanding our role as American citizens today. Understanding how America's character was formed—how it was defined by a love of liberty, a fierce independent spirit, and an unyielding commitment to defend our rights—is key to ensuring its future.

It is my hope that readers will come away from this book, not just with a greater understanding of the events that shaped our nation, but also with a greater appreciation for our nation's character. I also hope that readers will want to learn more. *America's Beginnings* synthesizes the work of many historians, and I hope provides citizens with the basics of what they need to know about the colonial and revolutionary periods. But this book is just a beginning. I urge readers to delve deeper into America's past, perhaps using this book's bibliography as a starting point. And I urge readers, informed and inspired by a deeper understanding and appreciation of how America's character was shaped, to embrace fully the privileges and responsibilities of American citizenship.

ACKNOWLEDGMENTS

My thanks go to Paul Aron at Colonial Williamsburg, a fine editor and author in his own right. It was a pleasure collaborating with Paul from the inception of the idea through the final edits. Kevin Kelly, an excellent historian at Colonial Williamsburg, went through the manuscript with a fine tooth comb, pointing out errors large and small. I would like to thank the support of the Colonial Williamsburg Foundation generally. As an educator, I appreciate the excellent work of the Foundation in educating citizens. It is a national treasure and a local treat for me as a resident of Williamsburg. At Rowman & Littlefield, Jon Sisk was a fervent supporter of the book and shared our vision of it.

I would like to thank my family for their support while writing this book. I also want to thank all the citizens I've met across the country while lecturing about my books and other historical topics. Across the political spectrum, Americans are a vibrant lot of patriots who may disagree on policy but continue to agree on fundamental principles.

I dedicate *America's Beginnings* to my dearest friend, Bruce Khula, who is the firmest and most thoughtful patriot I've ever met.

I

SETTLEMENT

· 1 ·

Lost Colony

$\mathcal{I}$n the 1500s, the Spanish Empire became fabulously wealthy because of the discovery of gold and silver in the Americas. The English were relative latecomers to the New World. Queen Elizabeth I did not use the government to pay for an empire. Instead, she allowed private investors to create joint-stock companies to fund English privateers who hunted Spanish treasure ships. The companies could also establish colonies.

In 1576, Sir Humphrey Gilbert published a pamphlet urging English explorers to find a Northwest Passage to the lucrative Asian trade and to colonize the coasts of North America. Gilbert died during an expedition to Newfoundland in 1583, and a year later Sir Walter Ralegh received an exclusive patent to settle on the Outer Banks of North Carolina. On April 27, 1584, Ralegh sent two ships to the Outer Banks. They determined Roanoke Island was a suitable site for a privateering base, took two Indians back to England with them, and promoted the venture to English investors to fund another voyage.

Queen Elizabeth supported the effort by releasing Ralph Lane from service in a colonial pacification program in Ireland. Lane was made governor, but the expedition was led by general and admiral, Sir Richard Grenville. On April 9, 1585, a fleet of seven ships and some six hundred men sailed for Roanoke. A storm scattered the fleet and sank one of the smaller pinnaces, so the ships stopped at Puerto Rico to build a new one. That task accomplished, they resumed their voyage and landed at Roanoke in late June. Most of their food was lost when a ship was driven against a bank, and the 107 men who stayed behind to establish the colony were forced to live off the land until supply ships could return.

Meanwhile, the Roanoke colonists built houses, a storehouse, and a diamond-shaped fort with a firing step. Grenville, upon his arrival in England, encouraged Ralegh to send supplies. Ralegh had already acted. In June, he had sent a relief fleet with supplies, but it was diverted to Newfoundland at the request of Elizabeth to warn the fishermen there of a sea war with Spain. The priority was to protect and defend the emerging British Empire.

Lane's men in Roanoke were drawn from across English society. There were poor workers, gentlemen, skilled artisans, miners, and geologists. In addition to setting up a base for privateers, they also searched for gold, the Northwest Passage, and commodities to trade in England. Scientist Thomas Harriot was appointed to survey and map the area. Painter John White faithfully represented images of the flora and fauna of the area as well as the Indians.

The local Algonquian Indians were essential to the survival of the colony, helping them plant corn and set up fishing traps. The Algonquians lived in villages and engaged in agriculture and hunting. They were guided by the leadership of *werowances* and redistributed goods among all. Although the English colonists sought to treat the natives well and avoid what they considered Spanish atrocities, Lane had also learned in Ireland not to appear weak. In the spring of 1586, relations soured between the two peoples and the Algonquian broke the fishing weirs and withdrew their support of the English simply by moving away. Finally, Pemisapan, the chief of the Roanoke tribe, planned an attack against the English. Lane caught wind of this and took the offensive. The settlers attempted their own surprise attack when they met with Pemisapan. At a prearranged signal, they managed to kill several Indians. Permisapan fled, but one of Lane's men chased him through the woods and slew him.

On June 8, Sir Francis Drake arrived at Roanoke after a highly successful privateering campaign against the Spanish. Drake agreed to provide boats, men, supplies, and guns to Governor Lane's colony. However, before Drake could set sail, a mighty storm blew into the area and raged for three days. Several small boats and pinnaces were destroyed and the larger ships had significant damage. Because of the terrible destruction and continuing difficulties feeding themselves, Lane and the colonists yielded to what they imagined to be the inevitable and returned with Drake's fleet to England. At the time, three men were investigating the interior. They were abandoned to their fate. Hundreds of Africans and Indians liberated from the Spanish were also left behind.

Three supply ships under the command of Grenville arrived only a few weeks after Lane and his men left. Had Grenville not been seeking Spanish prizes on his return trip to Roanoke, he might have reached the colony in time to convince Lane to remain. As it was, finding a deserted colony, Grenville left fifteen men with artillery and supplies and the goal of finding the missing Roanoke colonists, then he sailed back to England.

Despite the failure of the expeditions, promoters in England still abounded. Harriot and Richard Hakluyt argued that the long-term success of colonies depended on them being agriculturally self-sufficient, providing raw materials to England, and acting as markets for finished British goods. This economic model, known as mercantilism, was based on colonies trading exclusively with the mother country. With this mercantilist model in mind, a third expedition to Roanoke was organized under the leadership of a new governor, John White. These colonists were comprised of a number of families who would receive land grants and be governed by a council. In May 1587, three ships sailed from England. They arrived by late July and moved into the houses the settlers of the Lane colony had built. By the end of August, the settlers begged White to return home and ensure they received adequate supplies. By November 1587, he and Ralegh were organizing a supply fleet for the spring of 1588. The sailing of the Spanish Armada against England delayed the trip until April. When the ships were severely damaged in privateering battles, they limped back to England.

White did not sail again until 1590, when he was allowed to go aboard some privateering vessels that finally reached Roanoke in August. The settlers were gone. They had left two messages—CRO on a tree and CROATOAN on a palisade post—but neither with the prearranged distress signal. White searched for them but could not find them. The Spanish, hoping to destroy the colony, also looked for them and were also unsuccessful. Finally, twenty years later, the Jamestown settlers investigated the matter and never found any definitive answer. The members of the Lost Colony were never found.

Some historians have speculated that the colonists might have been attacked by Indians or Spaniards. Others think they joined with Indian peoples, and intermarried. This would explain why later colonists reported seeing some Indian children with English features.

· 2 ·

Jamestown

$\mathscr{I}$n 1603, James I ascended to the throne upon the death of Elizabeth I. One of his first acts was to sign a peace treaty with Spain to end the destructive and costly sea war. James, however, still authorized joint-stock companies to establish colonies in North America. In April 1606, adventurers John Smith, Bartholomew Gosnold, and Edward Maria Wingfield won a royal patent from the king. The Virginia colony was not envisioned as a base for privateering, but was expected to show a healthy return for investors.

On December 20, 1606, the *Susan Constant, Godspeed,* and *Discovery* sailed from England with 104 settlers who were interested in finding gold, a Northwest Passage, and valuable commodities to send back to England. The instructions and leaders for the colonial council were kept secret until they landed. Storms delayed the voyage by several weeks and dissensions arose aboard the ships. John Smith was clapped in chains for apparently starting an insurrection among the men. On April 26, 1607, after stops in the West Indies, during which Smith was almost executed, the ships finally went ashore in Virginia. After foiling an Indian attack, the colonists opened their instructions and surveyed the James River for a suitable place to settle. While they were exploring they encountered many friendly Indians and erected a cross to claim the land for God and the king.

On May 14, the settlers chose a marshy peninsula on Jamestown Island as the site for their colony. It was a defensible position against both Spanish ships and Indians. There seemed to be plentiful game for food and timber for building, and the river was a deepwater channel for ocean-going ships. The colonists set up shelters and fishing nets. After several were injured and killed by a surprise Indian attack, they decided to build a fort. Satisfied that the colonists were off to a good start, Christopher Newport, captain of the *Susan Constant*, held a farewell dinner and sailed back to England on June 22. He carried a letter from the council requesting a second expedition with supplies.

Despite some initial successes, the colony was devastated that summer. Nearly half of the colonists perished, primarily from saline river water which caused salt poisoning. Dysentery and typhoid also raged through the population causing lethargy, suffering, and death. The colony also experienced squabbles for power among its leaders and Wingfield was removed from the presidency. The English were heavily dependent upon the Indians for survival.

Captain Smith went on many expeditions to get corn from the Indians through a combination of trade and force. He was captured and taken before Opechancanough, a powerful leader and brother to Wahunsonacock (Powhatan), chief of some thirty tribes of the Powhatan peoples. Smith also met and was impressed by Powhatan. When his warriors held down Smith and acted as if they were about to club him to death, Powhatan's young daughter Pocahontas supposedly intervened and saved his life (though it may have been a ritualized ceremony Smith did not understand). When he was released and returned to Jamestown, Smith was tried and convicted for the death of two of his men. On January 2, 1608, he very nearly hanged again. Newport fortuitously reappeared with nearly one hundred settlers and provisions for the struggling colony, and pardoned Smith. Although Smith was saved, the colony was nearly lost. A few days later, a fire burned Jamestown to the ground, even though it was the dead of winter.

Over most of the following year, the colonists searched for gold. Newport went on a fruitless search for gold before departing again in April. Smith complained, "There was no talk, no hope, no work, but dig gold, wash gold, refine gold, load gold." Meanwhile the men were hungry and miserably cold. Smith put the men to work rebuilding the fort, storehouse, and church. He also went on a voyage of discovery, seeking gold and the Northwest Passage, but was unsuccessful. Many more died the following summer. Then, on September 10, Smith was elected president and instituted military discipline to restore order and industry. When Newport returned to Jamestown in October, he brought seventy settlers, insufficient provisions, and a desire to go on yet another elusive quest for gold, this time to the foot of the Blue Ridge Mountains. In December, Newport departed for England with a few commodities but no gold.

Smith did what he could to save the colony from disaster. He organized the men into work gangs to plant crops and maintain the town. He laid down the rule that they would "work or starve." He traded with the Indians for corn, barely keeping the colonists alive with his precious cargoes. The men were dispersed to different locations around the area but still the conditions were only minimally alleviated.

Back in England, the members of the Virginia Company reorganized their charter. Joint-stock shares in the company were cheaper and more affordable. The company was given total authority, free of royal control, and the members decided to elect a governor with near absolute power over the colonists. They still hoped for a large return on their investment in the form of gold, raw materials, and the Northwest Passage. Skilled artisans were recruited and a massive propaganda campaign was started to stimulate investment. So far, though, no gold had been discovered, nor any commodity of any great value. The hopes of the company members would be dashed, and in Virginia, things got worse.

· 3 ·

Starving Time

𝓘n June 1609, eight ships and five hundred colonists set sail from Plymouth Sound bound for Virginia. Onboard the 250-ton flagship *Sea Venture* was the leadership for the fleet and the Jamestown colony: interim governor Sir Thomas Gates, admiral Sir George Somers, and vice-admiral Christopher Newport. The instructions for the colony were also on the *Sea Venture*. If the ship were lost, it might spell disaster for the colony, which still hovered on the brink of collapse. The colonists had consumed most of the provisions that had already been brought across the Atlantic, and the summer brought more salt poisoning from the James River and a lethargy that meant no crops were planted. The colonists desperately needed the fleet's provisions.

The ships were taking a new route that took them more directly across the ocean. After suffering still winds and a ship fever that claimed thirty-two people, a massive hurricane struck the fleet and tossed it about for nearly three days. They were slammed by a "swelling, and roaring as if it were by fits, some hours with more violence than others, at length did beat all light from heaven; which like an hell of darkness turned black . . . so much the more fuller of horror." Torrential rain, screaming winds, and mountainous seas threatened to sink the fleet. Their sails were shredded, and their masts were cut away. A pinnace was lost and the *Sea Venture* took on water because her seams were jarred loose.

The exhausted crew and passengers on the *Sea Venture* desperately pumped the water out of the hull for three long days and nights. It was a losing battle. The ship took on water faster than they could pump it out. They thought they would perish when they suddenly spied the island of Bermuda, which they called the "Isle of Devils."

Nearing the island, the *Sea Venture* stuck fast between two rocks. Those on board rescued what supplies and parts of the ship they could, then rowed ashore before the *Sea Venture* was destroyed in the surf. On the island the castaways found wild hogs and other food, while they scoured the island to find materials to build another ship. They were scared and divided; some men mutinied against Gates's authority. But they were also innovative and determined.

Meanwhile, four damaged ships of the fleet limped into Jamestown in mid-August, followed by two others a week later. The hundreds of new colonists caused numerous problems for Jamestown. They arrived with very few edible provisions, and so many additional people placed huge demands on the contents of the storehouses. There was also a leadership vacuum with the colony's leaders and instructions presumed lost at sea. The colony had to be divided up, with some men sent up to the Falls at Richmond and others downriver to other plantations. John Smith struggled to retain the presidency and was challenged by the newcomers. Moreover, tensions with the Indians drove Powhatan to flee with his stocks of corn, while others attacked Jamestown and kept the colonists restricted to the fort.

In the early autumn, Smith's enemies ignited his powder bag while he slept on a ship. This caused an explosion which lit his clothes on fire and burned his "flesh from his body and thighs, nine or ten inches square in a most pitiful manner." Smith only survived by jumping into the river and dousing the flames. His enemies then apparently attempted to kill Smith in his bed. By October, Smith—who had sought to instill discipline and to keep the colonists alive—ignominiously departed the colony and returned the England.

The English at Jamestown had very little food during the harsh winter. Some tried to mutiny and steal vessels and were never heard from again. Others went to the Indians to trade for food but were killed in retribution for earlier aggressive actions. Powhatan and his warriors surrounded Jamestown and plucked off straggling colonists and their livestock, further depleting food stocks. The starving settlers were reduced to eating "serpents and snakes, and to dig the earth for wild and unknown roots." They also consumed horses, dogs, cats, mice, and even leather. They may have even resorted to cannibalism. More than 160 perished at Jamestown from the dreadful conditions.

In Bermuda, the survivors of the shipwreck, using rescued parts of the *Sea Venture* and local materials, ingeniously built two small boats which they aptly named *Deliverance* and *Patience*. They reached Virginia in May 1610, to the great surprise of the colonists. The former castaways were in turn shocked at the pitiable condition of the settlers at Jamestown who "looked like [skeletons], crying out 'we are starved, we are starved.'" Since Governor Gates had few provisions to alleviate the deplorable conditions, he decided to have the colonists abandon the settlement and make for Newfoundland and then England.

Just as they were sailing downriver, they were met by an advance party of Governor Lord De La Warr's relief voyage of three ships carrying 150 settlers and supplies. De La Warr ordered Gates's fleet back to Jamestown and instituted a strong regime of law and order and rules with harsh punishments to restore discipline and rebuild the ruined colony.

Although he was partly successful in repairing the colony, De La Warr could not save the colonists from disease and more than one-third perished. Many in the Virginia Company withdrew their investment and the colony struggled to endure. Almost eighty percent of the settlers who went to Jamestown died within a short period of arriving in the colony. Nearly a decade after its inception, the promised wealth of the colony was not materializing. An alternative model had to be found or the English would have to abandon their efforts to build an empire in North America.

· 4 ·

First Representative Legislature
in Britain's New World

*T*he first settlers at Jamestown had little say in who ruled them. The Virginia Company selected a council of thirteen men to govern the colonists in America. The men and even the leaders themselves were not privy to who was chosen until they arrived on Virginia shores. The settlers did, however, carry with them the traditional rights and liberties of Englishmen stretching back to the Magna Carta.

For its first decade, the Jamestown colony was poorly governed and rights were not always protected, even if theoretically guaranteed. With the colony teetering on the edge of collapse, the settlers endured military discipline. At times, a sense of individualism and autonomy led colonists to disobey harsh orders. The leadership of the council was constantly at odds, and several presidents were deposed. The political chaos was compounded by the failure of the colonists to produce almost any return on the investment made by the company.

In 1618, as the colony was finally beginning to thrive and expand, the company instructed governor-elect George Yeardley to introduce "just laws for the happy guiding and governing of the people." The company was concerned about the image the public had of the military governance of the colony. It did, after all, seem to be contrary to the spirit of English laws and liberties. The company created a council of state whose function was to advise the governor in the discharge of his duties. Its members would still be selected by the company in London. The company also directed that the council of state comprise one of the houses in the new General Assembly. The other house, however, was a

12

House of Burgesses with representatives chosen by the free inhabitants of eleven towns, hundreds, and plantation settlements. The "liberty of a General Assembly being granted to them," the free men would be able to "execute those things, as might best tend to their good."

The General Assembly was to convene once a year unless extraordinary circumstances necessitated it being called into session more frequently. Its task was to make laws for the public good and order the colony's affairs. The governor could veto legislation made by the Assembly. The company retained power of the colony and had the authority to approve laws. The laws of the colonial government were quite reasonably required to be in harmony with the laws of the mother country. The company sought stability that would generate additional investment and settlers willing to move to Virginia. But, the company also recognized the traditional principle upon which consensual government was founded: that "every man will more willingly obey laws to which he hath yielded his consent." Thus, the first representative legislature in Britain's New World was born in Jamestown, a decade after the initial colonists landed and just as the Pilgrims were planning to sail for North America.

The General Assembly gathered for the first time on July 30, 1619. The twenty-two burgesses assembled in the Jamestown Anglican Church. They prayed and then took an oath of loyalty to the king of England. As the Assembly convened, it first agreed to certain parliamentary procedures and accepted its members. Petitions for redress and complaints were heard. The Assembly considered Indian relations and its mandate to convert them to Christianity. As would be the case in Puritan Massachusetts, the colonists were required to keep the Sabbath and attend services of the official religion. The Assembly regulated the price as well as the quality of tobacco, but it also sought to encourage the development of diverse crops and commodities. The Assembly laid down rules regulating personal behavior—excessive drinking, idleness, and gambling.

On August 4, the assembly met as a court and heard charges against Englishman Henry Spelman, who had lived among the local Indians and served as an interpreter. The court heard testimony that Spelman disparaged the governor in front of Opechancanogh. The interpreter had allegedly said that there was a new governor coming "greater than this that now is in place." Spelman was charged with conspiring with the

Indian chief and endangering the colony by making it appear weak in front of the Indians. Spelman was found guilty and faced the death penalty, but the court recognized that his skills were indispensable. He was sentenced to serve the governor as an interpreter for seven years.

When King James revoked the company's charter in 1624 and made Virginia a royal colony the following year, the representative Virginia Assembly survived the change. With ownership of private property and appreciation for individual initiatives in work, greater freedom had also evolved. All these freedoms laid the foundation for the success of the Jamestown colony. The colonists would continue to claim the rights of Englishmen during the Glorious Revolution decades later and during the American Revolution.

· 5 ·

First Africans

*D*uring the first decade of the colony, the Jamestown settlers sought easy wealth and engaged in little productive labor, preferring to wait for supplies from England or steal from the Indians. The men shared goods from a common storehouse and had no incentive to work hard and plant food. Instead, they spent their time in a fruitless search for gold. They exported little of value back to England and required fleets of provisions, which were quickly consumed, and new immigrants, many of whom died, for the colony to survive. Investors had dumped more than £50,000 into the venture with almost no return.

Many innovations finally turned the colony around and contributed to its success. First of all, John Rolfe introduced a milder and sweeter variety of tobacco from the West Indies. After the discovery of America and tobacco, smoking had become all the rage in England. Addicted Londoners smoked incessantly in fashionable public spaces, even causing King James I to publish a tract, *A Counter-Blaste to Tobacco*, harshly condemning the habit. He called tobacco a "noxious weed" and smoking a "vile and stinking a custom" that ruined English manners. The company discouraged the colony from relying on the single crop. Nevertheless, Rolfe's plant was far superior to the rough taste of the local variety and soon was in great demand from England.

In 1614, the first significant Jamestown tobacco crop was exported to England. By 1618, approximately 20,000 pounds were sent. The figure doubled in 1620 and then nearly doubled again a few years later. One Jamestown official complained about the "market place, and streets, and all other spare places planted with tobacco." The colony had found a

15

profitable commodity at last, and it proved to be the colony's salvation. It fundamentally altered the shape of Jamestown, leading to new settlements along the James River, creating a demand for labor, and encouraging new settlers to seek opportunity in North America.

Ignoring the claims of the Indians, Virginians used the promise of abundant land to attract new settlers. Immigrants to the colony received land grants of at least fifty acres for settling in Virginia. They could gain additional acreage (called a headright) by paying the passage of poorer individuals from England who wished to indenture themselves as servants for five to seven years. These poor of England found opportunity in the New World for social mobility and land ownership. They were responsible for feeding themselves and, in private property, they had an an incentive to work hard.

Africans had a very different experience in colonial Virginia. In the summer of 1619, two privateers, a Dutch man-of-war, the *White Lion*, and the English ship, *Treasurer*, attacked the Spanish *São João Bautista* off the coast of Mexico and stole some African slaves transported from Angola, Africa. When the *White Lion* arrived in Jamestown, the Dutch ship bartered "20 and odd Negroes" for provisions.

By 1625, the African population was twenty-three. Two and a half decades later, the number had barely risen to three hundred, still a small percentage of the total inhabitants of the colony. Since slaves were more expensive to purchase than English servants, and since the mortality rate for Africans was so high, the colonists preferred to import more Englishmen and women.

Though Africans in these first few decades were slaves when they arrived, Virginians did not necessarily keep them as slaves. Most were probably treated as indentured servants and required to work a length of time before they were released. Even when they were considered slaves, they were usually allowed to work off their involuntary service and purchase their freedom. Either way, English servants and Africans worked, slept, and ate together. They both suffered harsh punishments as well.

There were also many Africans who were free. Despite some recognition that they were different because of skin color and religion, free Africans were readily accepted into the community as the equals of English settlers. Moreover, the two peoples freely intermingled socially. Free Africans bought, sold, and raised cattle, and owned their own land, on which they raised tobacco. Anthony Johnson, for example, owned

250 acres of land. They readily adopted the ethos of the English settlers—ownership, liberty, and a strong streak of individualism.

Free Africans of some means who owned property purchased indentures and won headrights for servants to work their land and raise tobacco. The African property owners even purchased other African slaves and allowed them to purchase their freedom. Africans regularly appeared in court and sued English colonists in disputes over property. By 1660, 950 Africans lived in the colony but still comprised only 3.5 percent of the population.

Over the decades, the rights of Africans were slowly eroded and differentiated from the other colonists. A racially-based system of hereditary slavery developed in the second half of the seventeenth century, driven by the massive demand for labor to meet the needs of tobacco planters exporting millions of pounds of tobacco to England at a time when English migration to Virginia declined. By 1705, hereditary African slavery was enshrined in law with harsh slave codes regulating behavior.

The enslavement of Africans in the American colonies was a part of the wider Atlantic slave trade. Ultimately, approximately five percent of the almost ten million Africans carried to the New World went to British North America. Most slaves worked—and died—in the disease-ridden and horrific working conditions of the sugar plantations of the Caribbean and South America.

· 6 ·

Mayflower Compact

 $\mathscr{K}$ ing James I and his Anglican bishops harried the dissenting Protestants known as Puritans, forcing their ministers to conform to official doctrine. Some Puritans decided England was morally bankrupt and the Church of England irredeemably corrupted by pompous clergy and Roman Catholic ritual. Their chronicler William Bradford wrote, "Religion has been disgraced, the godly grieved, afflicted, persecuted, and many exiled, while others have lost their lives in prisons and others ways; on the other hand, sin has been countenanced, ignorance, profanity, and atheism have increased, and the papists have been encouraged to hope again." The "Separatists" decided that they must leave England and form a separate church. After a frustrating decade in Holland, these Pilgrims, as they were called in Holland, decided America was the place to establish their church.

The Pilgrims worked through the Virginia Company to receive a grant from the king for land around the Hudson River. After securing a ship, passengers, and provisions, the Pilgrims left England for America. During the summer of 1620, the Pilgrims sailed from London to Southampton to rendezvous their 180-ton ship *Mayflower* with the much smaller and leaky vessel, *Speedwell*, and pick up some "Strangers" (non-Pilgrim settlers). The two ships put into Dartmouth for repairs to the *Speedwell* and were then held up by contrary winds. In late August, they finally began sailing and were a few hundred miles off the coast when the *Speedwell* sprang another leak. They returned to Plymouth where they ditched the smaller vessel and crowded onto the *Mayflower*, leaving some people behind. On September 6, the *Mayflower* sailed for America "with a prosperous wind, which continued for several days."

The passengers on the *Mayflower* suffered the usual affliction of sea-sickness and the ship was damaged in fierce storms. They committed "themselves to the will of God, and resolved to proceed." Following the common sea lanes, they sailed across the Atlantic Ocean and into the Caribbean, then rode the Gulf Stream northward. By this time, they were experiencing the debilitating symptoms of scurvy and prayed for land. After sighting Cape Cod on November 9, they sailed around for a few days avoiding perilous shoals and trying to decide whether to make for the Hudson.

While they were still on board the *Mayflower*, the Pilgrim men convened to form a covenant with God and each other.

The founding political document read:

> In the name of God, Amen. We whose names are underwritten, the loyal subjects of our dread sovereign lord, King James, by the grace of God, of Great Britain, France, and Ireland, King, Defender of the Faith, etc., having undertaken for the glory of God, and advancement of the Christian faith, and honor of our king and country, a voyage to plant the first colony in the northern parts of Virginia, do by these presents solemnly and mutually in the presence of God, and of one another, covenant and combine ourselves into a civil body politic, for our better ordering and preservation, and the furtherance of the ends aforesaid and by virtue hereof to enact, constitute, and frame, such just and equal laws, ordinances, acts, constitutions, and offices, from time to time, as shall be thought most meet and convenient for the general use of the Colony, unto which we promise all due submission and obedience. In witness thereof we have here underscribed our names at Cape Cod, 11th of November, in the year of the reign of our sovereign lord, King James of England, France and Ireland the eighteenth, and of Scotland the fifty-fourth. A.D. 1620.

From a practical point of view, the Pilgrims were facing a hostile environment and would have to cooperate to face the dangers that awaited them. They did not know whether the soil would be fertile or the native peoples friendly. They bound themselves to obey laws for their survival and common good. They believed that everyone pursuing their own individual desires would spell disaster.

But, the Pilgrims also laid down certain principles of government throughout the document. They were pursuing the glory of God and the advancement of Christianity. Although they were religious Separatists, they pledged their fealty to king and country. The laws would enforce the Ten Commandments and be in harmony with biblical precepts.

The leaders were assumed to be the wisest and most virtuous among them, and the people would be required to submit to their just authority. Having a stable government and orderly society would enable the Pilgrims to focus on creating their churches in the New World.

But the Mayflower Compact was also an expression of civil consent to republican government. From the very beginning, Americans sought to rule themselves. In that sense, the Mayflower Compact was a forerunner of the Declaration of Independence and the Constitution.

On November 11, "having found a good haven and being brought safely in sight of land," some went ashore and "fell upon their knees and blessed the God of heaven who had brought them over the vast and furious ocean, and delivered them from all the perils and miseries of it, again to set their feet upon the firm land and stable earth, their proper element." They reconnoitered the area in their shallop for the next month, encountering Indians. They then decided upon a permanent settlement at Plymouth, where they began building shelters.

Their survival was by no means secure. They had landed in New England during winter with inadequate provisions. Bradford described the deadly winter: "In two or three months' time half of their company died, partly owing to the severity of the winter, especially during January and February, and the want of houses and other comforts; partly to scurvy and other diseases. . . . Of all the hundred odd persons, scarcely fifty remained, and sometimes two or three persons died in a day." But survive they did, and by adhering to their compact they laid a foundation for future settlers.

· 7 ·

City Upon a Hill

$\mathscr{I}$n March 1629, investors received a royal charter for the Massachusetts Bay Company. This was also the beginning of a turbulent political period in England. King Charles I dissolved Parliament and did not call it again for eleven years, leading to a bloody civil war between royalist and parliamentary forces. In October, the company elected Puritan lawyer John Winthrop its governor, and he organized the first fleet of what would be a massive migration to New England during the following decade.

In April 1630, almost four hundred settlers sailed for America aboard the 350-ton flagship *Arbella* and her three sister ships. Some shared the Pilgrims' vision of establishing a separate church in America. Others were Puritans who sought to build a pure church in the wilderness that would serve as a model to reform the Church of England. When this occurred, they planned to return to their beloved England.

Many who went to Massachusetts were from the eastern counties of England and were of middling rank. They were usually skilled artisans and were highly literate, valuing education and reading the Bible. Many came as families, and they came with a strong work ethic, unlike some of the gentlemen adventurers in Virginia. In Massachusetts, they usually owned land and worked a self-sufficient farm. Massachusetts Bay developed no significant cash crop, attracted relatively few servants, and did not require the labor of large numbers of African slaves.

Sometime before they sailed, during the voyage, or shortly after they landed, Governor Winthrop delivered a sermon entitled, "A Model of Christian Charity." Winthrop laid down the scriptural basis for their political and social covenant: "That every man might have need of other, and from hence they might be all knit more nearly together in the bond of brotherly affection." The public good had to "oversway all private respects" so that the community could survive and build a godly commonwealth. This was accomplished by "mutual consent."

If they upheld the covenant, the colonists would receive providential blessings. On the other hand, if they violated it grossly, the colonists would endure God's punishment.

The covenant had wider implications than for just Massachusetts Bay, Winthrop explained. The Puritans were going to be an example of piety and virtue for England and the world. In words that over time assumed broader meaning, Winthrop stated: "We must consider that we shall be as a city upon a hill, the eyes of all people are upon us; so that if we shall deal falsely with our God in this work we have undertaken and so cause him to withdraw his present help from us, we shall be made a story and a by-word through the world."

This idea of an American "city upon a hill" became more secularized during the American Revolution. The Puritan ideal of a pure church setting the example for England evolved into the ideal of the American republic as a beacon of liberty for the world. And the Puritan character evolved into what we think of as the Yankee, and to some extent the American, character, with its insistence of the value of individuality.

The new colonists had to face more pedestrian issues when they landed in June 1630. They lived in tents and wigwams while establishing towns and suffering the effects of scurvy and other diseases. Thirteen other vessels followed Winthrop's fleet into Massachusetts that year. They experienced a tough winter. Fever spread through their camp and the colonists starved until a supply ship appeared in February 1631. More than two hundred perished, and the fortitude of the survivors was deeply shaken. Winthrop believed that God had "purged out many corruptions" and "striped us of our vain confidence." Many returned home.

Reports of the struggle to stay alive in Massachusetts Bay hardly stemmed the tide of immigrants over the next decade. Nearly two hundred ships voyaged across the Atlantic carrying between 14,000 and 20,000 settlers intent on reaching Massachusetts Bay. Despite casualties, the healthy climate and the fact that many of the colonists came as families led to a rapid increase in population. Although only 7,000 people immigrated to the north during the subsequent six decades, by the turn of the century the population of New England numbered some 100,000 people.

The General Court met quickly in late August 1630, and created a government that enforced the Ten Commandments and suppressed heresy. Governor Winthrop and other members of the council granted the franchise to all male citizens who were church citizens. There were annual elections of representatives of the General Court. The colonists moved from Boston to new towns that sprung up across the landscape. They formed dozens of autonomous congregational churches based upon church covenants among those who passed a test of their religious conversions. Town meetings of the people dominated local political rule. Schools were established in the towns. This migration stretched into Maine and New Hampshire while the more conservative went into Connecticut and the Separatists toward Narragansett Bay.

· 8 ·

Indian Uprising of 1622

The tobacco revolution in Virginia led to the expansion of English settlements throughout the fertile farm lands along the James River from
Elizabeth City westward to the Falls. The colonists recommitted themselves to the conversion of the Indians and set up schools for them with
funds from England. Some Indians even came to live among the colonists. In January 1622, the governor reported that Virginia was "in very
great amity and confidence with the natives."

The Powhatan chief Opechancanough, who had replaced Powhatan when he lost his authority and then died in 1618, professed peace to
the English. The new leader visited Jamestown, intimated that he was
interested in Christianity, and proclaimed that he sought no revenge
when his greatest warrior, Nemattanew, was killed in March 1622. He
promised that the death "should be no occasion of the breach of the
peace, and . . . the sky should sooner fall than peace be broken." This
was an elaborate ruse.

The colonists did not understand the ominous significance of
Opechancanough assuming the name of Mangopeesomon or his brother
Opitchapam changing his to Sasawpen. Name changes were a common
signal of war among the native peoples. Opechancanough was deeply
angry that the settlers had driven off his people and taken prime Indian
lands on the James. The war chief knew that he could not directly confront the English in a set-piece battle. He spent years forming an alliance
of native peoples and plotting to murder the English, destroy their colony, and drive them out of Virginia.

On March 22, 1622, hundreds of Indians (including five hundred to six hundred Powhatan and Pamunkey warriors) arrived at various settlements, as they frequently did to trade deer, turkeys, fish, and other foodstuffs. After casually interacting with the English in their homes, gardens, streets, and fields, the Indians suddenly grabbed farming implements, knives, axes, clubs, and other makeshift weapons. The Indians killed men, women, and children. They mutilated some bodies and carried off some prisoners who were presumably executed. Livestock were killed to deprive survivors of food and towns were burned. In total, 347 colonists were murdered that day at more than two dozen sites.

Some settlements had received advance warning that saved them, though no general warning could be given. In others, wounded men and frightened women and children managed to grab weapons and put up a hasty defense, eventually driving off their attackers. The grisly task mostly completed, the Indian warriors melted back into the woods. In many places, only a handful of inhabitants were left alive. Shocked colonists quickly moved into fortified areas when the Indians came back in successive days and razed a few settlements.

The attack was as dreadful as Opechancanough intended. "The land is ruined and spoiled," one colonist cried, "We live in fear of the enemy every hour . . . for our plantation is very weak, by reason of the dearth, and sickness." The Indian chief had predicted that the death of nearly one-third of the settlers and the resulting difficulties would cause them to depart. A few months after the attack, he stated, "Before the end of two moons there should not be an Englishman in all their countries."

The Indians had scored a decisive victory, but the Virginia Company secured the use of thousands of old weapons and pieces of armor and sent them to the colony. The company instructed the governor and the colonists to wage a war of annihilation against the enemy Indians, "surprising them in their habitations, intercepting them in their hunting, burning their towns, demolishing their temples, destroying their canoes, plucking up their [fishing] weirs, carrying away their corn, and depriving them of whatsoever may yield them succor or relief."

The colony dispatched raiding parties against the Indians throughout the summer and fall, unleashing great destruction of their own. The English destroyed villages and cut down the corn in the fields before torching them. The Powhatan warriors attacked some Englishmen in small ships the following spring, killing several and seizing their armor and weapons, but the English succeeded in a deadly ruse themselves.

They feigned friendship with Opitchapam, but gave his people poisoned wine, followed up by several volleys from their weapons.

After the murderous and destructive raids by both sides, they met in a rare set-piece battle that was bound to favor the well-armed and armored English, regardless of Indian numbers. In July 1624, roughly a thousand native warriors attacked sixty Englishmen in open battle. Over a two-day battle, the Indians fought bravely but suffered staggering losses compared to the light English casualties. The victorious colonists took the Indians' corn.

The war that lasted from 1622 to 1624 had dramatic consequences for both the English and the natives around the James River. The Powhatan Empire was driven off its lands. The English population and hunger for land to plant tobacco continued to grow rapidly. And, in 1624, after almost seventeen years of struggle and great mortality, the Crown revoked the Virginia Company's charter. The following year, the new king Charles I, having decided trade and commerce was too important to leave in the hands of a private company, made Jamestown a royal colony.

Another Indian attack in 1644 would kill five hundred more, but by that time, the Virginia colony was large enough to absorb the losses and continue to expand.

·9·

Dissents of Anne Hutchinson and Roger Williams

$\mathscr{P}$uritan Massachusetts faced two dissenters whom the authorities considered serious threats to the religious orthodoxy and social unity of the colony. They charged a man named Roger Williams and a woman named Anne Hutchinson on several counts, found them guilty, and banished them. Both these dissenters had criticized the Puritans for not being orthodox enough in their faith.

Roger Williams immigrated to America in 1631. He was already a renowned preacher and the Boston church offered him a position as teacher. Williams promptly declined the position because the church refused to renounce its ties with the Anglican Church. After a short period in Salem, Massachusetts, he went to the Separatist church at Plymouth. When that church did not prove itself sufficiently Separatist in Williams's eyes, he returned to Salem and taught there in 1635.

Williams was harshly critical toward the idea that the Puritans were a chosen people. He stated that they received no special revelation. He believed in a separation of church and state because he did not want the government to enforce church law and corrupt the church. Likewise, he did not want ministers to sully themselves with matters of the world. He opposed allowing the unconverted to listen to sermons or to take the Lord's Supper because they, too, corrupted the services. He supported liberty of conscience because he believed that government should not coerce belief, though he also maintained that religious beliefs other than his own were gross errors. In late October 1635, the General Court banished Williams. By January of the following year, he started the settlement of Providence, Rhode Island.

Anne Hutchinson was born Anne Marbury in England. Her father, Francis Marbury, was a clergyman who was persecuted and imprisoned for his Puritan views. In 1634, Hutchinson and her husband followed minister John Cotton to Boston. This was a patriarchal society, but women were the spiritual equals of men. Women could be members of the Elect, who underwent a conversion experience to God's grace and were saved. Groups of pious men and women met in private homes to discuss the weekly Bible reading, repeat the minister's sermon (on which they often took notes), read the catechism, pray, and sing psalms. These meetings were endorsed by the clergy.

Beginning in 1635, Hutchinson offered a weekly prayer meeting at her home. At first, only a handful of women attended. By 1636, she had attracted a rather large following with as many as sixty or seventy people, including several men, attending the meetings. She soon ran afoul of the town's authorities.

Hutchinson was not supposed to actually teach theology, which was a ministerial (and thus, male) prerogative. Moreover, she was not to challenge the social order or the ministers. Many ministers heard that she was criticizing them for teaching a covenant of works for salvation. A basic tenant of Puritanism was that God's grace was rooted in faith and could not be earned through works. The Elect had been predestined for salvation since the beginning of time. Good works, many Puritans believed, were a sign that God's grace had come into a person who was thus a "Visible Saint."

Hutchinson argued that salvation was completely rooted in faith, not good works. This challenged the teachings of the ministers and upset the social order, particularly because she was a woman preaching to men. Reverend Thomas Weld feared her audience was "being tainted" and might spread "the infection" of heresy to others. Another minister, Hugh Peter, lamented that she "stepped out of [her] place." Peter thought she "had rather been a husband than a wife; and a preacher than a hearer; and a magistrate than a subject."

In the summer of 1637, the Massachusetts court ordered Hutchinson not to lead prayer meetings, but she ignored the edict. The ministers also met with her to discuss her errors and convince her to repent, but they could not. In November, she was formally brought before the General Court and questioned by the authorities. She resisted every effort of the authorities to elicit an admission that she had wrongly criticized the ministry.

A the end of the trial, Hutchinson defiantly addressed the court. She stated, "Take heed how you proceed against me. For you have no power over my body. Neither can you do me any harm, for I am in the hands of the eternal Jehovah my Savior." She also claimed to have had a direct revelation from God, which provided the governor and the General Court with all the justification needed to convict and banish her.

After the General Court found her guilty, Governor Winthrop read the sentence: "Mistress Hutchinson, the sentence of the court you hear is that you are banished from our jurisdiction as being a woman not fit for our society, and are to be imprisoned till the court shall send you away." She was placed under house arrest away from her family. Meanwhile, the forty-six-year-old woman was pregnant with another child.

Hutchinson's ordeal was far from over. In mid-March 1638, she was dragged before the Boston congregation on charges of heresy. She continued to say that the ministers preached false doctrines. Most of the congregation, except for a few supporters who were effectively silenced, supported the charge. Her former ally, Reverend Cotton, admonished her for her beliefs: "Your opinions fret like a gangrene and spread like a leprosy, and infect far and near, and will eat out the very bowels of religion, and hath so infected the churches that God knows when they will be cured!" Because of the "great hurt" and "great dishonor" she did the church, the congregation assented to her excommunication.

Hutchinson moved with her husband, most of her children, and some followers to the island of Aquidneck, near Roger Williams's Providence Plantation. Later she moved to New York. It would be decades before the modern conception of religious liberty would come to New England.

· 10 ·

Pequot War

$\mathscr{P}$uritan and Indian traders were both shrewd. Relations could be tense, especially when the colonial traders were iniquitous or brusque. Captain John Stone, for example, was a violent drunk who drew knives on public officials and cursed them publicly. He also kidnapped and held some Indians hostage. In 1634, he was murdered by the Pequot and western Niantic Indians. In July 1636, another unscrupulous trader, John Oldham, was murdered while sailing off Block Island. Although the attack was perpetrated by Indians associated with the Narragansett Indians, it was pinned on the Pequot, especially when Uncas, the sachem (leader) of the Mohegan, informed John Winthrop that the Pequot were preparing for war. (Uncas hated the Pequot and tried to stir hostility with the Puritans, so this was probably a fabrication on his part.) Six other traders during the 1630s were slain, and the fears of the colonists grew.

The Puritans wasted little time formulating a response to Oldham's death. Massachusetts Bay authorities issued an ultimatum to the Pequot with a series of harsh demands. First, the Pequot would be required to pay the large sum of 1,000 fathoms of wampum to the colonists. Second, they would have to turn over the suspected murders to the Puritans for prosecution. Finally, the Indians would have to turn over children as an indemnity against future violence.

When the Pequot Indians rejected the terms, the Puritans decided to attack their village on Block Island. On August 22, 1636, the abrasive Puritan leader, Captain John Endecott, assembled ninety volunteers and sailed for Block Island, reaching it just before dusk. A group of fifty or sixty Indians launched a barrage of arrows against Endecott's party. The

30

Puritans escaped mostly unscathed and drove off their enemy with musket fire. As they marched across the island, there were some sightings of
Indians but no further major encounters. The frustrated Puritans burned
the wigwams and corn fields of a village they found. They withdrew the
following day.

The Pequot responded by laying siege to the Fort Saybrook garrison
in Connecticut on the Connecticut River under the command of Lion
Gardiner who desperately appealed to the colonial assembly for supplies
and a relief column. Some of his men tried to protect nearby cornfields
that were the fort's main food supply. They were captured, tortured, and
executed. The Pequot went to the Narragansett for an alliance against
the English, but the Narragansett spurned the offer. Had they aligned
themselves, they would have presented a major threat to the existence of
the New England colonies. In October 1636, the Narragansett agreed to
an alliance with the Puritans. The Mohegans, Massachusetts, River
Tribes, and later the Mohawks, followed the Narragansetts' lead..

In April, the Pequots raided Wethersfield, Connecticut, where they
killed nine settlers, roasting one alive and slaying the others with arrows.
Other Pequot raids killed as many as three dozen, which represented
more than 5 percent of the colony's settlers.

That month, the Massachusetts Bay Colony called for militia volunteers. The following month, Connecticut declared war on the Pequot.
Captain John Mason of Connecticut marched out with ninety colonists,
seventy of Unca's Mohegans, and hundreds of Narragansett warriors.
Captain John Underhill soon joined him with twenty men from the Saybrook garrison. At dawn on May 26, the colonists and their Indian allies
formed concentric rings around the perimeter of the Pequot fort at Mys-
tic, with the English in the inner ring and their allies forming the outer
ring. Within the fort were between four and seven hundred Pequot, who
were soon reinforced by another one hundred fifty warriors.

The attack commenced at dawn at two points. The Pequot put up
a ferocious defense and kept the attackers at bay. To gain the upper hand,
Mason picked up a flaming brand and threw it into the village, setting
the buildings on fire. Hundreds of Pequot were killed. The English lost
only two men dead but took twenty casualties and their Indian allies suffered 50 percent casualties. Although the colonists' allies participated in
the killing, some objected that the slaughter was simply too much.

In the coming months, the English and their Indian allies pursued remaining Pequot Indians. The English caught a group of two hundred Pequot, killed two dozen men, and divided the women and children among other Indian tribes. On July 14, another few hundred Pequot were discovered in a swamp near New Haven, Connecticut. The combined colonist-Indian army executed eighty warriors and again dispersed the women and children. The Pequot sachems begged for an end to the war and, on September 21, 1638, agreed to a peace treaty at Hartford.

The Pequot were routed as a culture and people, though they slowly reorganized within a few decades. The Puritans believed that God had sanctioned the war and their victory over the Pequot. Underhill stated, "We had sufficient light from the word of God for our proceedings." Chronicler William Bradford wrote, "They gave the praise thereof to God, who had wrought so wonderfully for them, thus to enclose their enemies in their hands and give them so speedy a victory over so proud and insulting an enemy." The war established what would become a standard American strategy: use overwhelming force and advanced technology and tactics against the enemy.

II

COLONIES

· 11 ·

King Philip's War

In the wake of the Pequot War, relations between the Indians and English in New England were generally harmonious. However, the cultural and economic interactions of the two people altered the Indian way of life. The English colonists spread westward, putting pressure on Indian lands. Moreover, the English unwittingly spread diseases among the Indians that caused a significant decline in their population. The Puritans opened up schools and sent missions to the Indians to convert them to Christianity and European-style civilization. At some Indian "praying towns," Christian Indians lived apart from their people. Even trade, which often benefited native peoples who acquired European goods and guns, made them dependent on those goods and disrupted their traditional trade networks.

When Massasoit, grand sachem of the Wampanoag, died in 1661, his son, Wamsutta (or Alexander) became sachem. He died the following year. His brother, Metacom (Philip), then became the sachem. Although there was a great deal of suspicion between the English and the Wampanoag, an uneasy peace lasted until 1675.

In late January 1675, John Sassamon was murdered shortly after warning governor Josiah Winslow that the Wampanoag were preparing for war. Sassamon was a Christian Indian who had fought for the English, attended the Harvard Indian school, and preached Puritan doctrine. In 1660, he had returned to his people and served as Philip's secretary and translator. He had recently come back to English society to live and was then found dead under the winter ice on Assawompsett Pond. His death was thought accidental until Patuckson, another Christian Indian, testified that he witnessed three Wampanoag murder Sassamon. In June, the three accused Wampanoag—Tobias (a counselor to Philip), Tobias' son Wampapaquan, and Mattachunnamo—were taken to Plymouth for trial. The three Indian defendants faced a jury of twelve Englishmen and an auxiliary Indian jury which concurred with murder convictions and death sentences. On June 8, the three were hanged, but Wampapaquan's rope broke and he survived. He was given a reprieve after he confessed that Tobias and Mattachunnamo were in fact guilty of the crime which he claimed to witness but not participate in. Nevertheless, after nearly a month, he was also executed. Hearing rumors of war and knowing the effects of the trial on Philip, the colonists sent a few embassies and letters to the Indians to assuage their anger. These efforts were for naught.

On June 20, Philip's warriors assaulted the Plymouth colony frontier settlement of Swansea and burned some of the houses. A young English boy shot an Indian on June 23, and the next day nine settlers were killed. Plymouth governor Josiah Winslow quickly sent two hundred militiamen to Swansea. Massachusetts governor John Leverett dispatched three more negotiating parties to avert war, which allowed Philip and his men to escape the clutches of a colonial force sent into his territory.

Other frontier towns were assaulted and burned while the colonial army pursued Philip's forces. The English caught up to the Wampanoag army by the end of July and took them by surprise, killing two dozen Indians. Philip and his warriors eluded capture but had to leave behind nearly one hundred women and children whom the English sold into slavery.

Meanwhile, Indians besieged the town of Brookline and drove the frightened residents into the crowded garrison house. The Indians surrounded the colonists and picked them off with muskets while trying to set the stronghold on fire. A relief force arrived after a harrowing forty-eight-hour siege and drove off the attackers. The town was utterly razed and had to be abandoned.

The Indian attacks in Massachusetts increased in the ensuing months—Deerfield was hit and three hundred homes in Springfield were burned. Philip's daring actions attracted additional Indian allies to his cause. By December, the Narragansett people were increasingly belligerent and might have participated in some of the frontier raids against the English settlers. The New England colonies of Massachusetts Bay, Plymouth, and Connecticut sent a thousand-man army into Narragansett country. On December 19, the army assaulted a large, fortified Narragansett village in the Great Swamp, Rhode Island. It was a bloody engagement, and over six hundred Narragansett were killed, but English losses were heavy and the army effectively incapacitated. The Narragansett were now firmly in the enemy camp.

The attacks continued throughout the winter, with the towns of Pawtuxet and Framingham struck at the end of January 1676. Other western Massachusetts towns—Lancaster, Medfield, and Weymouth—were attacked in February. Mary Rowlandson, a minister's wife in Lancaster, was taken prisoner and held captive for months until she was finally ransomed. She later wrote an enthralling captivity narrative, *The Sovereignty and Goodness of God*, about her experiences.

In March, Groton, Northampton, and other frontier settlements were laid waste, while a Plymouth Colony militia company was nearly wiped out in an ambush. The attacks continued in April, when as many as five hundred Indians assaulted the town of Sudbury. By the spring, virtually the entire Massachusetts western frontier was evacuated.

The apparent strength of the Indians in launching these raids masked problems that would soon turn the tide of war in favor of the colonists. The Indians were a highly mobile and effective fighting force, especially when the colonists fought in the style of Europeans in linear formations. However, this meant that the Indians could not remain in any single area to harvest fish or plant crops adequate to feed an army. The Indian warriors grew hungry and frustrated. Many eventually surrendered to the English.

The settlers were increasingly militarily successful. On April 3, Connecticut soldiers captured and executed one of the greatest Indian tacticians, Canonchet. In June, a combined army of New England militia surprised and killed one hundred Indians in the Connecticut River Valley. Major John Talcott and his Connecticut militiamen captured and killed almost two hundred Narragansett on July 2. The following day, eighty surrendered and were slaughtered. Major William Bradford, meanwhile, captured and killed hundreds more in Massachusetts, and hundreds of Indians surrendered to authorities in Boston. They faced execution or enslavement.

Philip could not escape the English forever. In early August, his wife and son were captured. On August 12, 1676, one of Philip's men betrayed him, revealing his location to the English. Captain Benjamin Church, who used Indian tactics against the Indian enemy, pursued Philip to a swamp near Mount Hope, where his force shot and killed Philip. The Indian leader's lifeless form was beheaded and quartered, and his head was sent to Plymouth to serve as a warning. Church's men soon forced the surrender of Anawan, Philip's brother and chief warrior, who was executed.

King Philip's War was the bloodiest war in American history to date. The war destroyed New England Indian populations and altered their way of life. Survivors moved further west or settled among the English.

· 12 ·

Bacon's Rebellion

$\mathcal{I}$n 1675, tensions between settlers and Indians were high in Virginia because of English westward expansion and trade disputes. In July, wealthy planter Thomas Matthew, who lived near the Potomac River, accused some Doeg Indians of trying to steal corn while trading and several men on both sides were killed. Local militia captains set off with a few dozen men to seek justice. Acting without orders from the government in Jamestown, they crossed the river into Maryland where they skirmished with a party of Doeg and killed twenty-four of the Indians. Virginia royal governor Sir William Berkeley ordered an investigation into the event, but his authority was flouted and ignored.

On September 26, a combined force of one thousand Virginia and Maryland militiamen surrounded a Susquehannock Indian fort on the Potomac. They parleyed with the Indian chiefs and then led them away for execution. The lower house of the Maryland general assembly fined Major Thomas Truman, who organized and led the expedition, a small amount. Governor Berkeley didn't punish the offenders from Virginia at all. In January, the Susquehannock had their revenge, sweeping into Virginia and killing thirty-six settlers along the frontier.

News out of New England about the brutal King Philip's War heightened fears of a general uprising of Indians. Berkeley ordered Sir Henry Chickeley to raise a force to march on the frontier but then countermanded the order because of a desire to avoid hostilities. Pressure built for an attack on the Indians, which would allow settlers to move onto their lands and relieve economic woes due to falling tobacco prices. The governor resisted the pressure. Even when he proposed raising five hundred militia to occupy the western forts, the taxes to support the army were unpopular. The assembly that met on March 7 declared war on all hostile Indians and those who abetted them or failed adequately to prove their fidelity to England.

Although no hostilities occurred that spring, rumors frightened residents on the frontier. A group of settlers from Charles City County petitioned Berkeley for a commission to lead a military expedition against the nearby Indians. When Berkeley denied it, the disgruntled farmers turned to Nathaniel Bacon. Bacon was in his late twenties when he arrived in Virginia in 1674. He was the son of a wealthy English squire and attended Cambridge University before briefly studying law. Because of some legal troubles, his father sent him to Virginia with the lordly sum of £1,800. He bought 1,200 acres along the James River and the governor quickly appointed Bacon to the council. The settlers turned to this impetuous young man for leadership.

In May, Bacon's army frightened off the Pamunkey Indians and then marched out to the Roanoke River near the North Carolina border. Bacon's soldiers wiped out a group of Susquehannock Indians with the help of Occaneechee Indians, but a dispute with their allies turned deadly and the English slaughtered the Occaneechee as well.

On May 3, the governor assembled an army of three hundred men to force Bacon to stand down but was unsuccessful in finding him. On May 10, Berkeley returned to Jamestown and issued two proclamations. First, he declared Bacon a rebel and relieved him from the council. His followers were to receive a pardon. Second, Berkeley called for new elections to the House of Burgesses and opened the election to all freemen. He also promised to allow citizens to express their grievances. When word arrived of the violence on the frontier, Berkeley was shocked and again labeled Bacon a rebel. Voters promptly elected Bacon to the House of Burgesses.

The Virginia Assembly convened on June 5, and the next day Bacon sailed to Jamestown with fifty armed followers. His ship was fired upon, and on June 7, Berkeley had him seized and arrested despite Bacon's bodyguard. When Bacon was brought before him, Berkeley declared, "Now I behold the greatest rebel that ever was in Virginia." Bacon's loyal band of men rallied to his cause and hundreds flooded the capital clamoring for his release. On June 9, Bacon offered Berkeley a written confession of his misdeeds and promised obedience. The governor repeated the words, "God forgive you, I forgive you," three times, pardoned him, and restored him to his seat on the council.

Berkeley promised Bacon a commission to fight the Indians but failed to deliver it. Bacon slipped out of the capital and gathered more than six hundred angry men. On June 23, they marched on Jamestown, where the governor could not raise an adequate defense. His men bellowed that they would get the commission or "else they would pull down the town or worse." They threatened the legislators with pistols, chanting, "We will have it! We will have it!" Bacon personally confronted Berkeley and screamed, "Damn my blood, I came for a commission, and a commission I will have before I go." Berkeley dramatically offered his breast to Bacon: "Here! Shoot me, before God, fair mark, shoot." Berkeley said he would rather have his hands cut off than do Bacon's bidding. The governor strode off, and an irate Bacon drew his sword and challenged Berkeley to a duel.

The terrified Assembly persuaded the governor to issue yet another pardon. Soon after, Bacon received news of Indian massacres on the frontier, and he and his army plunged back into the wilderness. While he was away, Berkeley tried to raise an army ostensibly to fight the Indians. Many suspected he meant to use it against Bacon and refused to volunteer. Bacon returned and arrived at Middle Plantation (later Williamsburg) on July 29, causing the governor to flee to the Eastern Shore.

This made Bacon the effective leader of Virginia. He issued his "Declaration of the People," denouncing "unjust taxes" and claiming the governor favored the Indians over the English. While he hunted Indians, Bacon also dispatched men to seize three ships in the James River. The rebels crossed the Chesapeake Bay but were defeated by troops loyal to the governor. Berkeley swore the rebels into the king's service, enlisted more locals, and sailed for Jamestown to confront Bacon.

On September 7, Berkeley arrived off the coast of Jamestown with an army of three hundred men. He faced a garrison of five hundred rebels. The governor pardoned all except Bacon and some other ringleaders. Many of the rebels deserted to Berkeley, who retook the capital. Bacon responded by offering freedom to slaves and servants if they would fight with him. He attacked with six hundred men, but the garrison was too heavily fortified. Bacon and his army lived off provisions from the governor's Green Spring plantation as well as other plantations and taunted the enemy to leave the protection of the fort. The men serving the governor grew disgruntled and their morale collapsed after a sally out of the fort failed miserably on September 15. Berkeley reluctantly withdrew his dispirited forces and Bacon burned Jamestown to the ground.

On October 26, 1676, Nathaniel Bacon died of dysentery and his rebellion fell apart. Most of his followers were pardoned, though a few leaders were hanged. By mid-February 1677, an English force of three warships and eight other ships carrying a total of 1,100 soldiers under the command of Colonel Herbert Jeffreys arrived to restore order. Jeffreys also brought a commission to serve as governor and instructions to ship Berkeley back to England. The government calmed tensions by reopening the Indian trade, though still blocking expansion for the time-being. It also garrisoned the forts and began ranger patrols along the frontier to protect settlers there. The virtual civil war between the representatives of the royal Crown and the fiercely independent Englishmen in Virginia was over.

· 13 ·

Glorious Revolution in America

 $\mathcal{I}$ n 1676, toward the end of King Philip's War, Sir Edward Randolph, the king's agent in Massachusetts, arrived for the first of his several missions to New England. Randolph was there to assess the allegiance of Massachusetts and its conformity to the laws of England. He reported that Massachusetts violated imperial trade laws (the Navigation Acts restricting colonial trade to England), denied religious liberty to Anglicans, coined its own money, and only allowed church members to vote. In short, the colony had grown too autonomous from the mother country. Randolph blamed the Massachusetts charter for the growth of the independent spirit and worked to have it revoked.

Massachusetts responded by dispatching a number of agents to the Crown to argue its case. In December 1683, the General Court voted to defend its charter in royal courts. The same month, a Puritan minister, Increase Mather, became one of the staunchest advocates of keeping the old charter. He addressed the Boston town meeting, stating that he hoped "there is not one freeman of Boston that will dare to be guilty of so great a sin," as submission to the loss of the charter and oppressive English control. Everyone at the meeting voted to preserve the charter.

Nonetheless, in 1684, the Crown won a court decision that resulted in revoking the Massachusetts charter and consolidating the five New England colonies, along with New York and East and West Jersey, into the Dominion of New England. On May 14, 1686, Randolph arrived with the king's commission for a new government. A week later, the General Court met for the last time. James II commissioned Sir Edmund Andros, former royal governor of New York, as the governor-general to administer the Dominion.

Andros arrived in December 1686, with two companies of soldiers to enforce his will. He made all of the greatest fears of the people of Massachusetts a reality. He ruled by a council and restricted town meetings to one per year. He forced the Puritans to accept Anglican services in a congregational meetinghouse. The Puritan ministers were also barred from earning salaries from tax money. Moreover, taxes were raised (without an assembly) to pay for Andros' £1,200 salary and for the soldiers stationed there. Andros challenged land grants made under the old charter and charged fees to grant them back to the owners. The governor-general also vigorously enforced the Navigation Acts through a new vice-admiralty court that operated without a jury. Cotton Mather quipped, "Foxes were made the administrator of justice to the poultry." He was not the only one who complained about the violation of political, economic, and religious liberties.

Minister John Wise led the people of Ipswich (in Essex County) in protesting taxation with their consent. He claimed the rights of Englishmen under the Magna Carta. Wise and thirty other leaders were arrested, tried and convicted under a special court of oyer and terminer. One of the judges proclaimed, "Mr. Wise, you have no more privileges left you than not to be sold for slaves."

Increase Mather resolved to travel to England for an audience with the king to plead the case of Massachusetts. When Mather publicly announced his intent in December 1687, Andros ordered him arrested. He was tried a month later but acquitted, and Andros had to pay the court costs. The minister delivered a farewell sermon and told the governor he was leaving, but Andros ordered him to stay. In late March 1688, Mather put on a wig as a disguise and sneaked aboard a ship bound for England. He met with the king on several occasions throughout the summer and fall but did not receive a new charter.

In late 1688, the Dutch prince William of Orange invaded England and James II fled to France. Early the following year, William and his wife, Mary Stuart, the daughter of James II, assumed the throne in a "Glorious Revolution." In February 1689, a Bill of Rights guaranteed a constitutional government and protected the constitutional rights of the people. A ship brought news of the Glorious Revolution to Boston in April, setting off an uprising against Andros and his government.

On April 18, mobs seized the royal frigate, *Rose*, and arrested Andros, Randolph, and other officials. Drums beat the call to war and almost two thousand militia men swarmed in from the surrounding countryside. The militia forced the surrender of the royal soldiers and sailors at the fort on Castle Island a few days later. Similar revolts occurred in New York and Maryland where the royal officials were arrested and sent back to England. The leaders of the revolution in Boston and Increase Mather in London proclaimed their loyalty to the new monarchs and sought reinstatement of the old Massachusetts charter.

In 1691, the people of Massachusetts received a new charter. The Crown would appoint the governor (and the lieutenant governor) who would have a veto over the General Court and could appoint his council. William III agreed to Increase Mather's request that the king make Sir William Phips governor. Religious toleration was granted to all Protestants and property replaced church membership as the primary requisite for suffrage.

Many Puritans were displeased by the acceptance of religious pluralism, but Mather praised the protection of ancient liberties. "By the new charter," he wrote, "great privileges are granted to the people in New England, and in some particulars, greater than they formerly enjoyed." The people of Massachusetts (and other colonies) had petitioned and revolted to preserve those rights and liberties. Actions that will be taken again just before the American Revolution.

· 14 ·

Salem Witch Trials

$\mathcal{T}$he Puritans believed in the Devil. The Devil intervened in human affairs and tricked men and women into practicing witchcraft. Witches flew to evil gatherings known as sabbats, where they mocked the Christian Sabbath. Witches caused misfortunes to happen to their enemies, usually in the shape of deformed animal births or inexplicable occurrences. They might have a familiar (a small animal such as a cat that did the witch's bidding) that suckled from a witch's hidden teat. Belief in witchcraft was widespread in Europe and America, even among the educated. Witches were a grave physical and spiritual threat to the community and were often put to death. In 1692, a devastating witchcraft outbreak gripped Salem, Massachusetts.

In February, nine-year-old Betty Parris and her eleven-year-old cousin, Abigail Williams, suffered strange fits and convulsions. Reverend Samuel Parris, Betty's father, called a doctor who was baffled by the girls' illness and gave his opinion that they were "under an evil hand." The girls said they were stuck with invisible pins in their flesh and blamed three women—West Indian slave Tituba, bedridden and old Sarah Osborne, and local pauper Sarah Good—for their torments. All three were arrested. During questioning, Tituba admitted to practicing witchcraft with Sarah Good.

Word of the girls' behavior spread. The number of afflicted mounted rapidly as did the accusations of witchcraft. The accused were questioned publicly in the meetinghouse, where the afflicted cried that they felt stabbing pains from the witches or could see specters—invisible to everyone else—flying around the room. The alleged witches were arrested and shackled in chains. Among those jailed were Rebecca Nurse, John Proctor, and Dorcus, the four-year-old daughter of Sarah Good.

On May 14, the new royal governor, Sir William Phips, landed in Boston. To hear the enormous number of witchcraft cases, he convened a Special Court of Oyer and Terminer. Among its members was Samuel Sewall, a wealthy merchant and legislative representative in the General Court. Governor Phips selected lieutenant governor William Stoughton to preside as the court's chief justice.

Not everyone believed the wild accusations. Reverend Cotton Mather, one of the leading ministers of Boston, believed in the existence of witches and evil spirits, but expressed a great deal of doubt about the outbreak. He warned against the use of spectral evidence in trials. Moreover, he thought the general practice of sinking a tied-up accused witch into water to see if the person drowned (and was therefore innocent) a barbaric "invention of Catholics and Episcopalians." He offered to take some of the afflicted into his home and remedy their ills through fasting and prayer.

The accused witches in Boston were taken to Salem for trial before the special court. On June 2, the court heard testimony against Bridget Bishop, which included spectral evidence and evidence of puppets stuffed with torturing pins. Bishop was found guilty and hanged. This miscarriage of justice so outraged the judge Nathaniel Saltonstall that he immediately resigned. A few days later, Increase Mather and several other ministers drew up a statement—"The Return of Several Ministers"—in which they expressed their dissatisfaction with the injudicious use of spectral evidence and demanded greater burdens of proof.

On June 29, with over one hundred accused witches incarcerated, the court convened for a second time and tried five of the accused in one day, including Sarah Good. Rebecca Nurse was found innocent but the verdict was sent back until it was reversed. Chief Justice Stoughton persisted in the use of spectral evidence despite the questions that had been raised. On July 19, the five convicted witches were executed in Salem. Good proclaimed her innocence and warned the judges from the scaffold: "I am no more a witch than you are a wizard, and if you take away my life, God will give you blood to drink."

On August 5, the judges met again and found six suspected witches guilty. Two weeks later, five hanged. Elizabeth Proctor was issued a reprieve because she was pregnant and it was thought wrong to take an innocent child's life because of the crimes of the mother. The accusations eventually reached into the upper echelons of Puritan society as Reverend Samuel Willard, members of Governor Phips's council, and Phips' wife were all named witches.

In early September, another half dozen accused witches were tried and convicted, though one was reprieved and one escaped from prison. Mary Easty, Rebecca Nurse's sister, begged for an end to the trials, not specifically for her own life, but so that "no more innocent blood be shed." On September 17, the court met for the last time and rendered nine guilty verdicts. Five confessed to be witches and thereby escaped the noose. Giles Corey, an elderly farmer, refused and was pressed to death by the weight of stones piled on top of him. On September 22, eight convicted witches from the two court sessions were hanged.

In early October, the ministers again rallied against the use of spectral evidence and called for an end to the trials in a short statement to Governor Phips. Cotton Mather's father, Increase, delivered a sermon in which he averred that, "It were better that ten suspected witches should escape, than that one innocent person should be condemned." On October 26, there was a call in the General Court for a day of fasting and prayer for divine guidance on how to proceed. Two days later, Phips met with Stoughton to discuss the fate of the court and, on October 29, Phips disbanded the court. Many in jail were released and Phips created an independent judiciary to handle criminal matters. The trials were halted and the lives of the jailed were spared.

In total twenty-two women and five men were tried and convicted before a halt was called to the proceedings. Nineteen people—fourteen women and five men—had been hanged, one man was pressed to death, and one woman (Osborne) died of natural causes while in jail.

Five years later, Samuel Sewall issued a public apology for his role as a judge in the witchcraft trials at his meetinghouse. His confession stated that he desired "to take the blame and shame of it, asking pardon of men, and especially desiring prayers that God, who has an unlimited authority, would pardon that sin."

Various proposals have been put forward to explain the Salem witch trials: the tensions between Salem village and the more prosperous neighboring town, women who broke with conventional sex roles, religious tensions among the denominations, the tensions over the loss of the charter, wars, even rye bread infected with a fungus. What's undeniable is that the Puritans of colonial Massachusetts believed in the existence of witches and the authorities allowed the accusations to multiply. Since then, the Salem witch trials have come to symbolize intolerance and persecution.

· 15 ·

Boston Smallpox Epidemic of 1721

$\mathscr{M}$alaria, yellow fever, and smallpox were only some of the diseases that routinely ravaged populations throughout the colonies. The epidemics occasionally had significant political impacts as well.

In late April 1721, a British warship, the H.M.S. *Seahorse*, unknowingly carried a sailor who had smallpox into Boston harbor. He transmitted the disease to his shipmates and at least one other person in town. The town authorities acted quickly to contain the disease. They quarantined the sick, but the disease spread through churches, shops, and homes and within weeks cases cropped up in every corner of Boston.

Cotton Mather sought to introduce an untested medical procedure—inoculation. As a Puritan minister, Mather might seem an unlikely figure to be found on the forefront of science, but he was also a member of the British Royal Society, the most august scientific body in the world. He had learned about inoculation from one of his slaves and from reading in the journal of the Royal Society about its practice in Greece and Turkey. Inoculation was done by creating an incision in the patient and placing into it the smallpox virus. Generally, the patient would get a mild case of smallpox and immunity for life. Five years before the outbreak of 1721, Mather had already resolved to "procure a consult of physicians to introduce [the] practice."

Initially, the doctors of Boston ignored the minister when smallpox struck the city. Finally, Mather persuaded one doctor, Zabdiel Boylston, to test out the procedure, which he successfully performed on his son and two slaves. Other patients soon came to Boylston to be inoculated. Meanwhile, almost one thousand people fled Boston in fear for their lives.

Many were outraged by a practice that seemingly spread disease. As Mather noted in his diary, "They rave, they rail, they blaspheme . . . And not only the physician who began the experiment, but I also am an object of their fury." The town authorities ordered Boylston to stop inoculating patients. He ignored them.

The doctors of Boston (who opposed inoculation) and the ministers (who favored it) wrote articles in the newspapers and pamphlets. This was a war of words in a town that valued words, especially those in the Bible. The doctors vehemently argued that inoculation, was dangerous, against scripture and the predestined will of God, and based upon the lies of slaves and pagans. The doctors refused to examine any patients or test the procedure in carefully regulated conditions.

The ministers replied that not intervening when people were sick negated the point of having doctors at any time. They rooted their arguments in natural law, arguing God gave human beings reason to discover scientific truths. Moreover, they pointed out, knowledge often came from non-Europeans and pagans. For instance, the Puritans had learned cures for rattlesnake bites from Indians. Hippocrates and Galen, upon whom the doctors depended for their medical knowledge, were pagans. Finally, the ministers argued that Africans were humans with reason and with knowledge Europeans had not yet acquired.

In August, two brothers, printer James Franklin and his brother and apprentice Benjamin, started a newspaper called the *New England Courant*. The newspaper served as a mouthpiece for the doctors and other writers. The newspaper published withering attacks on the new procedure as well as against the authority of the ministry.

As the inoculations continued, the death rate climbed among the general population—11 in July, 26 in August, and 101 in September. The epidemic reached its height in October with thousands of sick persons across the city and a staggering 411 deaths. So many people were infected that the disease was running out of human hosts.

The resentment against Mather, Boylston, and the Puritan ministers continued to grow. They were angrily confronted in the streets. By early November, an unknown person attempted to assassinate Mather in his home by throwing a bomb. The grenade crashed through a window of his home and split into two pieces without exploding. Attached was a note that read, "Cotton Mather, you dog, damn you! I'll inoculate you with this, with a pox to you!"

The smallpox epidemic in Boston ran its course by the end of 1721, but not before it killed almost 900 people in a city of only 11,000. Another 5,000 people suffered the disease and survived, most scarred and some blinded. Boylston successfully inoculated almost 250 people and lost only six patients, proving that it was a fairly safe way to immunize the population.

The furor over inoculation played a role in shattering the covenant that the Puritans made between themselves and with God. The attacks upon the ministers fractured Puritan society and a led to a decline of deference. The coming decades would see a further decline in deference— this time to the English king and Parliament.

· 16 ·

Great Awakening

$\mathcal{D}$uring the 1730s and 1740s, a wave of religious revivals stirred the colonies. Popular preachers sermonized before crowds of thousands in fields and streets. Their message was that individuals could and should repent. They sought to elicit a highly emotional response from listeners. Tens of thousands converted. New denominations struggled with existing churches for members and over the proper forms of Christian piety.

In 1739, a young, itinerant English preacher in his early twenties, George Whitefield, arrived in America and preached hundreds of times across the colonies. Whitefield delivered his sermons without notes. He was a brilliant orator, and he utilized his grand voice and dramatic gestures to move large crowds. A farmer recalled the electric effect that Whitefield's preaching excited in him: "When I saw Mr. Whitefield . . . a young, slim, slender, youth before some thousands of people . . . [it] put me into a trembling fear . . . and my hearing him preach, gave me a heart wound; by God's blessing: my old foundation was broken up." In Philadelphia, Whitefield befriended the agnostic Benjamin Franklin who was moved by Whitefield's sermons and saw potential profits to be made selling newspapers and pamphlets promoting him.

In New England, Reverend Jonathan Edwards produced a similarly emotional response. He stated, "Our people do not so much need to have their heads stored, as to have their hearts touched." His startlingly vivid sermons reminded the audience members of their depravity. In his *Sinners in the Hands of an Angry God*, he warned: "You are held over in the hand of that God, whose wrath is provoked and incensed as much against you, as against many of the damned in hell. You hang by a slender thread, with the flames of divine wrath flashing about it, and ready every moment to singe it, and burn it asunder." One listener testified that there was a "great moaning and crying through the whole house—what shall I do to be saved—oh, I am going to Hell."

The itinerant preachers brought an evangelical Christianity to thousands of converts. The ministers and the people who followed them were called "New Lights" as opposed to the "Old Lights" who followed the traditional Anglicanism or Puritan congregationalism. The New Lights saw themselves practicing a Christianity of individual conscience and grace. They searched their souls intensely and experienced a range of emotions from the deepest despair to the heights of joy. As Edwards wrote, "It was a very frequent thing to see an house full of outcries, faintings, convulsions, and such like, both with distress, and also with admiration and joy." God's grace, they argued, was open to all and welcomed young and old, male and female, black and white, slave and free. They preached Christianity to the slaves (previously it was feared that preaching to slaves would stir up their resistance to enslavement) and converted many youths and males who had strayed from their churches. The message of spiritual equality was a particularly radical one in a hierarchical society.

The New Lights consciously rejected what they saw as the excessive formalism of the Old Light denominations. The New Lights criticized the Old Lights for focusing on deference, order, harmony, religious duty, and good works and morality over piety. The carefully constructed Old Light sermons of highly educated ministers were dull and excessively rational, the New Lights argued; the sermons were wrongly aimed at the head, not the heart.

Whitefield charged, "The generality of preachers talk of an unknown and unfelt Christ. The reason why congregations have been dead is, because they had dead men preaching to them." Preacher Gilbert Tennent's attack was even more withering: "As a faithful ministry is a great ornament, blessing, and comfort to the Church of God . . . So, on the contrary, an ungodly ministry is a great curse and judgment." Reverend James Davenport even called them "unconverted hypocrites" and "the devil incarnate."

The Old Light ministers fired back, arguing that the New Lights caused divisions within churches, spread disorder in society, and were so emotional it bordered on insanity. One opponent of the revivals, Charles

Chauncy, defended the Old Lights. "The Gospel," he wrote, "doth not destroy reason and rational proceeding—the work of the SPIRIT is according to the nature of man, moves not in contradiction to it, but in an elevation of reason." He argued for proper deference and obedience to traditional ministers. The New Lights, he maintained, allowed lay commoners to interpret Scripture and undergo a conversion according to their own paths. He was particularly galled that the New Lights permitted women to preach to men, upsetting the social patriarchy. He cautioned that the New Lights threatened to engineer a social and religious revolution.

Traditionalists used their social status to pass restrictions on revival meetings and to persecute the practitioners of the new denominations. In 1742, for example, the Old Light critics successfully pressured the Connecticut General Assembly to ban itinerant preaching.

In Virginia, planter Landon Carter disdainfully noted, "Whitefield did but hum and buzz, and die away like the insect of the day." Nevertheless, the Great Awakening, as it became known, took hold in Virginia's Hanover County in the late 1740s with the preaching of Presbyterian minister Samuel Davies. Besides promoting emotional conversion and spiritual egalitarianism, the Presbyterians and Baptists, like the New Lights in other colonies, attacked the amusements and vices of gentry including gambling, horse-racing, and drunkenness. The government in Williamsburg required licenses for itinerant ministers, and then instituted an outright ban. In the coming decades, ministers espousing these new beliefs suffered public beatings, jailing, and horse-whippings even while preaching.

The enthusiasm of the religious revival ebbed within a few years time, but the new Christian denominations endured and greatly added to the pluralism of American religion, even though most colonies retained official churches. Moreover, the individual and democratic religious ethos of the evangelicals resonated through the politics of the American Revolution. The Great Awakening dealt a blow to social hierarchy and authority. In some ways, it harkened back to the congregationalism of the first Pilgrims to America, though in other ways, it was a revolutionary movement. During the Revolution, its ideas would meld with arguments for individual rights and political equality.

· 17 ·

Benjamin Franklin and the Lightning Rod

*T*he eighteenth century was called the Enlightenment, or Age of Reason, in Europe and the American colonies. Coming in the wake of the scientific revolution, it was a confident age. There were great hopes that the knowledge of the natural world would be discovered, classified, and organized into a coherent set of natural laws, leading to unbounded progress. These ideas were communicated among intellectuals through letters and journals and scientific societies such as the British Royal Society. Although many of the great theoretical scientific discoveries and political theories came from Europe, some practical discoveries came from the American colonies.

Benjamin Franklin, despite his role in opposing smallpox inoculation, was at the forefront of American science. He made meteorological discoveries about hurricanes and observations about the Gulf Stream in the Atlantic Ocean, he invented the Franklin wood stove and created a set of bifocals, and, most famously, he invented the lightning rod. Franklin never took out a patent or sought to benefit personally from his experiments. He was already wealthy from his publishing ventures and his other investments. His pursuit of knowledge for the benefit of humanity placed him squarely in the tradition of Enlightenment science.

In June 1752, Franklin and his twenty-one-year-old son, William, awaited a summer thunderstorm in Philadelphia. Franklin carried a silk kite fashioned with a crossbeam of cedar. There was about a foot of wire sharpened to a point atop the wood. The kite was attached to a few hundred feet of twine, which had a silk ribbon with a key tied to its length. Franklins stood indoors to keep the silk ribbon dry while they conducted their experiment.

56

They let out some of the string and the wind carried the kite aloft. The sky darkened. Suddenly, the pair noticed that the stray threads in the hempen string began to stand erect, signaling an electrical charge. The elder Franklin then brought his knuckle into contact with the key and felt an electrical spark. The electric charge flowed freely through the twine and the metal key gave off sparks. Benjamin Franklin had proven that lightning was electricity.

Actually, a comparable experiment (though not with kites) had been conducted shortly before then in France, but this should not diminish Franklin's role. He had not heard of the French experiment, and he was the one who turned the knowledge into a practical and lifesaving technology.

Franklin publicized his great innovation in the pages of his *Pennsylvania Gazette* and his *Poor Richard's Almanac*, where he wrote, "It has pleased God in his goodness to mankind at length to discover to them the means of securing their habitations and other buildings from mischief by thunder and lightning."

Franklin devised a way of protecting homes and public buildings from lightning strikes. He proposed driving a small iron rod of some three or four feet into the ground and connecting it by wire to another rod some six or eight feet above the building. "A house thus furnished," he promised, "will not be damaged by lightning, it being attracted by the points and passing through the metal into the ground without hurting anything."

During the summer of 1752, the world's first lightning rods were placed atop the Pennsylvania State House and the Philadelphia Academy. In September, Franklin erected a nine-foot-high lightning rod on the chimney of his own home. He developed a system of wires that were connected to the rod and dropped into the main staircase where it split into two and attached to two bells with a silk thread connecting them. On a stormy night, the bells would ring, sending shudders of fear through Franklin's wife Deborah. The sparks from the contraption even illuminated the stairwell.

Some scientists disputed Franklin's findings and he was also attacked by some Puritan ministers. One minister, Thomas Prince, claimed that lightning was a sign of divine displeasure with the sins of humankind. He argued that Franklin impiously wished to evade that judgment, which would incur greater wrath from above. Prince stated, "O! There is no getting out of the mighty hand of God!" Franklin believed, "Surely the thunder of heaven is no more supernatural than the rain, hail, or sunshine of heaven, against the inconvenience of which we guard by roofs and shades without scruple."

Franklin became the most famous colonist in Europe. He was routinely compared to the greatest scientists of the Enlightenment, including Isaac Newton. The Frenchman Jacques Turgot stated, "He snatched lightning from the sky and the scepter from tyrants." An envious John Adams later bemoaned the belief that, "Dr. Franklin's electrical rod smote the earth and out sprung George Washington." But this belief was not entirely unreasonable: Franklin would later use the fame he had acquired as a scientist to advance America's struggle for liberty on the global stage.

· *18* ·

Albany Plan of Union

$\mathcal{O}$ n May 9, 1754, the *Pennsylvania Gazette* published a political cartoon addressing the colonies' problems with the French and their Indian allies in the Ohio Country. The woodcut showed a severed snake, its parts representing the different colonies. The caption "JOIN, or DIE" was printed underneath and called for intercolonial unity. The cartoon was reprinted widely in other colonial newspapers.

The previous autumn, the British Board of Trade, concerned about poor relations with the Mohawk Indians, ordered that a conference be convened in New York to repair relations with the Indians. New York lieutenant governor James De Lancey obediently invited representatives of eight colonies to Albany. Representatives from North Carolina, South Carolina, and Georgia were not invited nor were Connecticut and Rhode Island (though they showed up anyway). Virginia and New Jersey chose not to attend.

Philadelphia publisher, scientist, civic improver, and politician, Benjamin Franklin, got himself appointed as a commissioner to Albany. In New York City for a short layover, he composed "Shorts Hints towards a Scheme for a General Union of the British on the Continent." His ideas would shape discussions during the coming weeks.

Twenty-three commissioners from seven colonies assembled on June 19. Gifts—the foundation for eighteenth-century diplomacy with the Indians—filling thirty wagons, were exchanged with the Iroquois Confederacy. The presents in this case included rum which was given liberally in the hope that inebriated Indians would cede disputed lands. The Connecticut and Pennsylvania delegations negotiated settler-favoring deals of millions of acres of land for only £2,000 and £400 respectively.

Cheating the Indians out of their land was hardly the way to win Indian trust and amity. On July 2, Iroquois chief Hendrick minced no words, dressing down the English. "Look at the French," he said, "They are men. They are fortifying everywhere. But—we are ashamed to say it—you are like women."

Hendrick continued, "You have thus thrown us behind your back and disregarded us." The delegates tried to placate the Indians with additional gifts and words of reassurance, though the Indians were hardly fooled.

De Lancey then shifted the meeting to consider several plans of cooperation among the colonies, of which Franklin's was only one. All of the plans shared a vision of a more united group of American colonies under some limited central authority for their mutual defense. The plans also all agreed the colonies would be subservient to British imperial authority. They did not contemplate a more independent America. The delegates appointed a committee to study the different ideas and draft a plan.

Besides the Franklin Plan, the committee examined a proposal brought by wealthy Massachusetts politician Thomas Hutchinson, which had the approval of the royal governor William Shirley. Hutchinson envisioned the creation of a northern and southern confederacy in America, each having greater power to combat the French in Canada and the West. The burden of war would also be distributed more equally among the colonies. Shirley was concerned that the Americans were becoming too independent of the mother country and wanted a union that was under the firm control of king and Parliament.

The committee ultimately produced a plan of union that closely resembled the proposal offered by Franklin. The congress debated it for more than a week in early July. The final Albany Plan of Union was a confederacy of eleven states (Georgia and Delaware were not invited). The colonies would have an intercolonial legislature called the Grand Council. It would have forty-eight representatives (elected by colonial assemblies), with representation based on tax revenues. No colony would have more than seven or less than two representatives. The legislature would have the power to raise armies, regulate western territories and trade, and levy taxes. The legislature would meet annually in Philadelphia. The plan included an executive (the president-general) who would, with the advice and consent of the Grand Council in London, have the power to make war and treaties. The Crown would appoint and fund the executive. Both branches of government would have three-year terms.

The Albany Congress unanimously agreed to its Plan of Union and adjourned on July 11. The plan held the promise that an intercolonial government could better coordinate a colonial-wide defense and have the means to go to war. However, the plan was unanimously rejected by the colonies. The colonies simply had too many differences and were unwilling to surrender their local prerogative to an intercolonial government. There was very little sense of a common bond or identity among the colonists. Small colonies feared being dominated by larger ones, and economic interests and land claims clashed. The plan also foundered in Great Britain, where some suspected that it might lead to greater independence for the American colonies. One member of Parliament warned, "an independency upon this country [is] to be feared from such a union." The Privy Council rejected the plan.

When war with the French and their Indian allies erupted, the British sent tens of thousands of soldiers across the Atlantic Ocean to fight for empire. The American colonists added thousands of troops, but the British commanded the armies and determined the strategy. The colonies remained disunited and subservient.

· *19* ·

Great Meadows

$\mathscr{I}$n 1753, the French built a series of forts in the Ohio territory, alarming the British and the American colonists. The British instructed Virginia lieutenant governor Robert Dinwiddie to assert England's "undoubted rights to such parts of the said river Ohio." The royal governor was to "repel force by force." He selected a young surveyor and adjutant general of the militia, George Washington, who had lobbied Dinwiddie for an assignment. Moreover, Dinwiddie ordered Washington to collect intelligence about the French forts. "You are to take care to be truly informed what forts the French have erected, and where; how they are garrisoned and appointed, and what is their distance from each other," the governor wrote.

Washington departed on October 31, plunging into the wilderness late in the season. He hired a young Dutchman named Jacob van Braam to serve as an interpreter with the French and a few men to tend to the horses and supplies. Washington traveled to Wills Creek in Cumberland, where he enlisted the services of the indomitable frontiersman, Christopher Gist, to guide the small party to the French. Gist led the party through thick woods, over mountain ridges, and across rivers. While they were traveling, Washington noted a possible defensive site near the Monongahela River that might serve as a fort. They soon came upon John Fraser's trading post and learned of recent French actions. Then, Washington and his team arrived at Logstown, a hunting cabin used by the Seneca chief, Tanaghrisson, known to the English as "Half-King." Washington offered the Indians customary gifts of wampum and tobacco. He then pushed his hosts for information about the French. Half-King agreed to accompany the young Virginian to help keep him safe during the journey, though the Indians disappointed Washington by not offering warriors to expel the French.

On December 4, the party reached Venango, where there was a fortified French house that Washington suspected would be the basis for building a fort. The commander, Captain Philippe de Joncaire, cordially welcomed Washington and invited him to stay and dine at the house. The tongues of the diners apparently loosened over wine and the issue of the French presence in the disputed territory was broached. Joncaire listened politely but then stated that it was "their absolute design to take possession of the Ohio, and by God they would do it, for though they were sensible, that the English could raise two men for their one; yet they knew their motions were too slow and dilatory to prevent any undertaking of theirs." The French were in the Ohio Country "to prevent settling on the [Ohio] River or waters of it, as they have heard of some families moving out in order thereto."

Joncaire nonetheless provided a guide for Washington to proceed to Fort Le Boeuf near Lake Erie, where they arrived on December 11. Captain Jacques Legardeur de Saint Pierre, the new commander of the post, welcomed the party and received Dinwiddie's letter. The letter complained about French encroachments on British lands and demanded "your peaceable departure." While Saint Pierre considered the letter, Washington was studying the "dimensions of the fort, and making what observations I could."

Claiming he lacked authority to respond to Dinwiddie's letter, Saint Pierre ultimately advised Washington to proceed to Quebec and give the letter to General Ange Duquesne de Menneville, marquis de Duquesne. But, he told Washington in no uncertain terms that, "I do not think myself obliged to obey" Dinwiddie's order. Having received his answer, Washington and his party left and began their long journey home. Washington and Gist battled the winter elements, getting swept away in an ice-clogged river in frigid temperatures. Their Indian guides even fired a few shots at them before disappearing into the wilderness. Washington finally made it back to Virginia and, on January 16, 1754, presented himself at the capital of Williamsburg to make his report.

Washington presented Dinwiddie with the reply from the French and also related the details of the embassy in his journal. Dinwiddie was impressed and asked the young man to prepare his journal for publication in order to sway public opinion. Meanwhile, Dinwiddie ordered Washington to raise one hundred militiamen, half the total force he intended to recruit. In mid-February, the governor convened the House of Burgesses earlier than scheduled to consider an appropriately bellicose response to what he interpreted to be French aggression. The legislature appropriated the relatively paltry sum of £10,000 to defend the entire frontier and provided the emissary £50 for his services.

The recruiting did not go well. Dinwiddie organized companies of volunteers with promises of land grants out west and tobacco. Washington thought that only derelicts had shown up and his army lacked the quality men he desired. Dinwiddie's plea to the governors of nearby colonies was relatively fruitless. The young and ambitious Washington was frustrated that overall command of the expedition was given to the more experienced Joshua Fry, and the young man was positively insulted when he learned that his pay would be less than that of a British regular of a comparable rank.

Since Fry was bringing his force separately, Washington received instructions that read he was to remain on the defensive but to "make prisoners of or kill and destroy" any French enemies if "attempts are made to obstruct the works or interrupt our settlements." With this in mind, Washington's small band of men set out from Alexandria on April 2, 1754, and was soon joined by Captain Adam Stephen's men, bringing the total to 159. Washington soon learned that the French had captured the unfinished English fort at the Forks of the Ohio.

Washington held a war council, which decided to march to Monongahela and approach Fort Duquesne. On the morning of May 27, Gist rode into camp and informed Washington that a party of fifty French was only one-half mile away. Washington assembled a party of colonists and Indians (led by Half-King) and quietly surrounded the opposing camp. Washington's men may have fired the first shots, sending the French scurrying for their muskets. Both sides exchanged heavy fire. The French commander, Joseph Coulon, Sieur de Jumonville, was wounded in action and surrendered. He was conferring with Washington when an Indian walked up and said, "Thou art not yet dead, my father," and struck the Frenchman dead with several hatchet blows. Nine other Frenchmen were killed after they surrendered. The outraged French claimed they were on a diplomatic mission, proving it with documents and arguing they were wrongly attacked.

Washington, having had his first taste of battle, related that, "I heard bullets whistle and believe me there was something charming in the sound." British king George II learned of the youthful remark and retorted that he would not "if he had been used to hear many."

Washington retired to the Great Meadows where his men built a hasty defensive position called Fort Necessity. It was a circular pallisaded fort around a stronghouse and defended by outside earthenworks. By June 9, Joshua Fry's contingent of 181 men arrived without their commander, who had died in a fall from his horse. A few days later, a company of British regulars under Captain Mackay arrived, though he refused to submit to Washington's command. On July 2, Half-King and his band of warriors melted away into the forest.

On July 3, the five hundred French troops and their Indian allies under the command of Captain Villiers (brother of the slain Jumonville) attacked Fort Necessity. They surrounded the fort, firing from the protection of the woods and high ground. Washington's placement of the fort in the clearing had been a militarily unsound decision. Additionally, a downpour ruined the English supply of gunpowder. After the onslaught, one-third of the English forces were dead and many were drunk from raiding the supplies of rum. Washington surrendered.

On July 4, Washington accepted the terms that the British had offered: the English could return home and Washington, because of a questionable interpretation of the French, unwittingly accepted blame for "assassinating" Jumonville. The nearly three hundred survivors marched away, and many simply deserted and went home. The first shots of the French and Indian War had been fired.

· 20 ·

Braddock's March

*I*n the wake of George Washington's humiliating surrender at Fort Necessity and the failure of the Albany Congress to unite the colonies, King George II was not about to let French aggression in the Ohio Valley go unpunished. The sixty-year-old, seasoned veteran Major General Edward Braddock was dispatched with two regiments of British regulars to expel the French from Fort Duquesne. This was part of a multi-pronged assault against French positions in Canada and on the American frontier. Braddock expected to defeat the French at Fort Duquesne, then roll up the Alleghenies and meet with victorious British troops at Fort Niagara. These struggles in America were part of the historical rivalry between the great powers of Europe and would soon become part of a world war.

Braddock disembarked at Hampton Roads in late February 1755, and his men arrived in mid-March. By April, he was meeting with the royal governors in Alexandria. He haughtily informed them of their duties to support the war effort and he refused to listen to arguments that colonial legislatures might not agree to fund it. Virginia and Maryland made numerous promises but were parsimonious with their supplies. In Pennsylvania, postmaster Benjamin Franklin secured the necessary supplies out of his own initiative. The printer quickly composed two broadsides appealing to the Pennsylvania backcountry to send horses, wagons, and teamsters to drive them. Within a few weeks, nearly 150 wagons and 500 packhorses were delivered. Smoked hams, Jamaican rum, Madeira wine, sugar, butter, tea, and coffee also arrived.

Besides the two regiments of British redcoats, Braddock acquired colonial troops and officers. An ambitious and proud George Washington resigned from the Virginia provincial army, when his rank was reduced to that of captain. He cajoled Braddock for a commission in the regular army. The British general agreed to take on the young man as an aide-de-camp volunteer because of his knowledge of the enemy and terrain.

At Fort Cumberland, Braddock accepted the troops sent by Maryland, Pennsylvania, and Virginia. He snubbed the Indians, whom he did not think very good fighters compared to well-armed and disciplined European troops. Rather than winning their alliance, he promised to occupy their land after he drove off the French. The Ohio Indians were furious and returned home to join with the French. Indeed, the Indians on the frontier were generally sympathetic to the French, who treated them better and were more interested in trade then conquest.

Braddock was left with virtually no Indian warrior allies to fight a major battle in the rough backcountry. On June 10, Braddock and his force of roughly 2,000 regulars and colonists began their march on Fort Duquesne. Braddock refused to take the Pennsylvania roads for his march and settled instead for the rough-hewn trails that Washington's small band had tramped across the previous year. Braddock's column, weighed down by artillery guns, wagon trains, and baggage, and having no clear path through the wilderness, made painstakingly slow progress. Men sickened and were barely able to travel, let alone fight. Washington himself battled disabling cases of dysentery and hemorrhoids. He barely caught up to the army before it engaged the French in battle.

On July 9, Braddock's army moved within a day's travel of Fort Duquesne. He sent out an advance guard of a few hundred men under Thomas Gage to probe the enemy defenses. The French commander of the fort, Captain Claude-Pierre Pécaudy Contrecoeur, who already had his scouts following the progress of Braddock's column, decided that same morning to send a sortie of 250 French and Canadian soldiers and 650 Indian allies. The two sides confronted each other and fired. The French officer in charge was dropped at long range by a musket ball. The Indian allies ran into the woods and flanked the British forces, attacking them from both sides and driving them back. The British advance party lost most of its officers as well as its discipline.

The fighting soon reached Braddock's main forces arrayed along the road. One survivor recounted, "The French and Indians crept about in small parties so that the fire was quite round us." They crawled through the brush and skulked from tree to tree, frustrating the British who formed themselves into ineffectual lines. The smoke, Indian war cries, and screams of the wounded added to the confusion. Braddock courageously rode through the ranks, with horses shot out from under him, vainly trying to rally his men. Finally, an enemy bullet penetrated his back and knocked him from his horse, gravely wounded.

Washington seized control of the situation. He tried to organize the headlong retreat, though he had two horses shot from under him and his coat was pierced with bullets. It was "as if we had attempted to stop the wild bears of the mountains." The British army and American militia finally broke ranks and fled, fearing they would be massacred and scalped. They ran for two days, closely pursued by enemy forces until the survivors reached safety. Braddock died along the way. Two-thirds of the soldiers in the British front column were killed or wounded. The French armies lost only a few dozen men.

The British suffered additional defeats on the American frontier until William Pitt effectively became the prime minister and helped turn the tide, escalating the war into a world conflict. The British moved northward and captured Forts Louisbourg and Niagara before General James Wolfe dramatically seized Quebec in 1759. Sir Jeffrey Amherst took Montreal the following year. The British victories spelled disaster for the French Empire in North America.

• 21 •

Royal Proclamation of 1763

$\mathcal{O}$n February 10, 1763, the peace treaty officially ending the French and Indian War in North America (also known as the global Seven Years' War) was signed in Paris. The British won Canada from the French, having defeated them in battles at Duquesne, Niagara, Quebec, and Montreal. The British ceded lucrative sugar islands in the West Indies and islands off Newfoundland surrounded by cod fishing grounds. The French ally, Spain, won back Manila in the Philippines and Havana after losing them during the war. The Indians believed that, with the French now expelled, their lands west of the Appalachian Mountains as well as their sovereign autonomy had to be defended against the British. An eastern Delaware prophet, Neolin, had visions of driving out the British invaders and exhorted Indians to live according to traditional and virtuous ways. Indian leaders, among them the Ottawa Pontiac, rallied their followers to make the vision a reality. They launched major assaults against western British forts at Detroit, Niagara, Sandusky, Pittsburgh, and others in May and June.

British commander Sir Jeffrey Amherst initiated a war of annihilation against the Indians. He ordered that his troops not take any prisoners and that every commander "defend his post to the last extremity; and to take every occasion he can of putting them to death." His successor, General Thomas Gage, continued the total war. The colonists refused British demands to send troops, but some Americans (such as the Paxton Boys in Pennsylvania) made independent and indiscriminate raids. The British ended the fighting by sending in two regiments of redcoats to turn the tide, lifting the siege of Detroit, and winning over the Indians as allies.

The British issued a proclamation to prevent any further troubles on the frontier. The government drew up a plan to reassure the Indians of British intentions not to violate Indian lands or sovereignty. In September, the plan was presented and debated. On October 4, the Board of Trade president, the Earl of Hillsborough, drafted a proposal that the Privy Council approved and King George III signed. The Royal Proclamation of 1763 attempted to relieve tensions between the colonists and Indians, impose order on the chaotic frontier, and organize the postwar North American British Empire.

The Proclamation created a West and East Florida from the territory acquired from Spain and a new province of Quebec in Canada, ruling them under British common law. The territory west of the Appalachian Mountains to the Mississippi River was reserved for the Indians. To prevent future wars with the Indians, American colonists were prohibited from settling west of the Appalachians. This was not just for the sake of the Indians. The British also feared that the colonists would fan westward across the newly acquired territory and identify and ally themselves with Britain's enemies.

The line was a firm but impermanent boundary for American settlement. In the Proclamation, the king announced his intention to make generous land grants to colonial veterans of the war. However, the colonial governments and royal governors were concurrently banned from granting any land themselves.

The colonists bristled at the impediments to their moving into western lands. Colonial land claims stretched to the Pacific, and the British seemed to be taking that property and giving all of it to the Indians. Backcountry settlers had a fiercely independent spirit. They ignored the edict and flooded into the frontier, often squatting on the land and improving it to claim ownership. The *Virginia Gazette* noted that "not even a second Chinese wall, unless guarded by a million soldiers, could prevent the settlement of the lands on Ohio and its dependencies."

Wealthier planters and merchants who speculated on Western lands also denounced the restrictions. Unlike squatters, the speculators had to show a clear title to the land. This was not possible, given the proclamation. Virginian George Mason claimed he had a "strict right" to tens of thousands of acres. George Washington was irate that the promised land bounties from the war were denied. He railed against colonial secretary

Lord Hillsborough: "I consider it in no other light than as one, among many proofs, of that nobleman's malignant disposition to Americans."

It wasn't just land policies that fueled American outrage. The presence of nearly 10,000 British redcoats that garrisoned the western forts rankled Americans who held the traditional English antipathy toward standing armies, seeing them as an instrument of tyranny. The clash between those troops and American colonists would erupt when the redcoats sought to suppress the colonists who were angry about taxes in the coming decade.

III

RESISTANCE

· 22 ·

Stamp Act

$\mathscr{A}$fter decades of "salutary neglect" during which the colonists governed themselves without much interference from the British, the Stamp Act of 1765 fundamentally altered the relationship of the colonies and the mother country. Prime Minister George Grenville proposed to raise revenue to pay for the defense of the frontier with the Stamp Act, which levied taxes on almanacs, legal documents, newspapers, and even playing cards. Parliament commenced debating the measure, and the American response was immediate. The American colonists were prosperous and enjoyed imperial trade networks and naval protection, and they paid relatively low taxes. But, the issue for the colonists would be one of principle, not purses.

In late December 1764, the Virginia House of Burgesses drafted the most forthright petitions to the king and Parliament remonstrating against the impending Stamp Act. Largely the work of Landon Carter, these documents appealed to the universal and constitutional principle of "freedom which all men, especially those who derive their constitution from Britain, have a right to enjoy." They conceived it to be "a fundamental principle of the British constitution . . . that the people are not subject to any taxes but such are laid on them by their own consent." Their property was the basis "for the genius of a free people" which could not be taken at will. Violating their natural and traditional rights made the colonists the "slaves of Britons."

In April 1765, the colonists learned that the king approved Parliament's Stamp Act. On May 29, in Virginia, young upstart Patrick Henry offered resolutions in the House of Burgesses that caused quite a "long and warm contest." The Burgesses, who had voted for the petitions the previous December, readily endorsed the first and second resolutions, which argued that the first settlers in Virginia brought with them the rights of Englishmen. Nor was the idea of the third or fourth—that the Virginians would tax and govern themselves—a source of contention. What stimulated a "most bloody debate" on the next day, in the words of a young observer named Thomas Jefferson who was then studying at the College of William and Mary, was the fifth resolution. It stated, "The General Assembly of this colony have the only and sole exclusive right and power to lay taxes and impositions upon the inhabitants . . . and that every attempt to vest such power in any person or persons whatsoever other than the General Assembly aforesaid has a manifest tendency to destroy British as well as American freedom." This resolution seemed to claim total political autonomy from Britain.

On May 30, the House was the site of a great debate and some fiery rhetoric. Henry bellowed defiantly, "Tarquin and Caesar each had his Brutus, Charles the First his Cromwell." He continued, either saying that, "He had no doubt but some good American would stand up, in favor of his country," or simply, "George the Third—" Either way, the implication was clear. Conservative Speaker John Randolph leapt to his feet and protested, "Treason!" Despite the verbal fireworks, the House passed all five resolutions, leading an outraged moderate, Peyton Randolph, to exclaim as he was going out of doors, "By God, I would have given 500 guineas for a single vote."

Henry put on his riding breeches and departed Williamsburg, giving the moderates the opportunity to rescind the offending fifth resolution. However, all the resolutions were printed in newspapers in other colonies as if they were all still in effect. The *Newport Mercury* and the *Maryland Gazette* even printed the more radical sixth or seventh resolutions, which may or may not have been presented in the House of Burgesses. The sixth read, "That his Majesty's liege people, inhabitants of this colony, are not bound to yield obedience to any law or ordinance whatsoever, designed to impose any taxation upon them." The seventh declared any who supported the Stamp Act was "AN ENEMY TO THIS HIS MAJESTY'S COLONY." Patriots in the other colonies were thrilled by Virginia's defiance.

In the late summer of 1765, ordinary citizens flooded the streets of Boston to protest the Stamp Act. On August 14, Bostonians found an effigy of Stamp Act collector Andrew Oliver hanging from a tree. That evening, an angry mob paraded the effigy to Oliver's "Stamp Office" and tore the building down in minutes. The crowd marched to Oliver's house, decapitated the effigy, and rifled the home. Its owner escaped in fear for his life. On August 26, Bostonians assembled again, shouting "liberty and property" as they advanced on lieutenant governor Thomas Hutchinson's house, which they plundered and demolished.

Similar incidents occurred across the colonies. Riots in New York and New Hampshire led several terrified stamp collectors to resign their positions before they or the stamps arrived in America. Rhode Island mobs hung effigies that called a stamp collector: "THAT FAWNING, INSIDIOUS, INFAMOUS MISCREANT AND PARACIDE." Collectors' homes were torn down in Newport, and angry citizens in Connecticut buried a collector alive until he resigned his position.

In October, twenty-seven delegates from nine colonies met in the most impressive example of intercolonial unity to date. Assembling in New York, the Stamp Act Congress declared, "It is inseparably essential to the freedom of a people, and the undoubted right of Englishmen, that no taxes be imposed on them, but with their own consent, given personally, or by their representatives." The delegates made clear that their only representatives were "chosen therein by themselves."

The purses of British merchants suffered when Americans stopped importing British goods in response to the Stamp Act. In February 1766, the new Rockingham ministry in England disavowed Grenville's policies and repealed the Act. However, Parliament also simultaneously passed the Declaratory Act, stating that it had the right to legislate for the colonies "in all cases whatsoever." The colonists had adamantly declared their rights, and the British had firmly asserted their authority. It was a recipe for further conflict.

· 23 ·

Townshend Acts

$\mathcal{I}$n the 1766 Declaratory Act, the Parliament had claimed its sovereign authority to govern the colonies and tax them at will. The British government was still in debt and still had to pay for maintaining a frontier army along the Proclamation Line of 1763. Chancellor of the Exchequer Charles Townshend proposed a series of new customs duties he predicted would raise annual revenues of more than £40,000.

Parliament passed the Townshend Acts by the end of June 1767, including taxes on lead, glass, paint, paper, and tea. It also established an American Board of Customs Commissioners to send officials to better administer America and ensure that the taxes were collected. Finally, Parliament suspended the New York Assembly for refusing to comply with the Quartering Act, which required the colonists to house and supply a standing army among them. The colonists perceived the army to be an example and instrument of tyranny.

The Townshend Acts met with widespread opposition throughout the American colonies. In late 1767 and early 1768, John Dickinson, a wealthy lawyer, landowner, and member of the Pennsylvania legislature, penned a series of *Letters from a Farmer in Pennsylvania*. They were reprinted in many colonial newspapers and collected into pamphlet form. They were arguably the most important pamphlets written on American rights until Thomas Paine's *Common Sense*.

While admitting Parliament's authority to regulate American trade, Dickinson severely criticized the taxes as an unconstitutional usurpation of American rights in the *Letters*. He asserted "a total denial of the power of parliament to lay upon these colonies any 'tax' whatever." If Parliament succeeded in "tak[ing] money out of our pockets without our consent . . . our boasted liberty is but a sound and nothing else," Dickinson wrote. He conceded British authority over America and pledged allegiance to the mother country but summoned his countrymen to "ROUSE yourselves, and behold the ruin hanging over your heads."

On February 11, 1768, the Massachusetts assembly adopted Samuel Adams' proposal denouncing the taxes. The taxes were "infringements of their natural and constitutional rights" because the colonists were not represented in Parliament and did not give their consent. This Massachusetts Circular Letter appealed to the other colonies to "harmonize with each other" and protest the taxes. That fledging unity soon took the form of nonimportation agreements (after some hesitation by each colony waiting for action by the others). By the end of the year, New York, Philadelphia, and Boston merchants agreed not to import British goods.

In April 1769, George Washington wrote to his neighbor George Mason enclosing a copy of the Philadelphia Association. Washington feared that "Our lordly masters in Great Britain will be satisfied with nothing less than the deprecation of American freedom." For Washington, American self-government was a moral principle: "That no man should scruple, or hesitate a moment to use arms in defense of so valuable a blessing, on which all the good and evil of life depends." Though he refused to advocate the use of arms at this early date, Washington averred that "their attention to our rights and privileges is to be awakened or alarmed by starving their trade and manufactures."

Mason agreed that American liberties were worth inestimably more than a few fineries and "comforts." He was promoting a Spartan frugality consistent with classical republican ideals. The pair hammered out a nonimportation agreement, and Washington took it to the House of Burgesses. On May 16, the House of Burgesses passed resolutions that asserted the "sole right of imposing taxes on the inhabitants of this his Majesty's colony and dominion of Virginia, is now, and ever hath been, legally and constitutionally vested in the House of Burgesses." The new royal governor, Lord Botetourt, responded: "I have heard of your resolves, and augur ill of their effect. You have made it my duty to dissolve you; and you are dissolved accordingly."

The Burgesses marched down Duke of Gloucester Street to the Apollo Room of the Raleigh Tavern where they appointed a committee to draw up a nonimportation agreement. The following day, they reassembled at the tavern and accepted a plan for nonimportation of British goods. The Association (which was modeled closely on Mason's draft plan) held that the Townshend Acts were "ill-advised regulations" and "unconstitutional" taxes. The Association was therefore refusing to import British goods, eschewing "all manner of luxury and extravagance." The "Daughters of Liberty" held spinning bees and made homespun clothing to replace imported fineries. Citizens proudly wore their homespun clothes as evidence of their patriotic simplicity.

In 1769 and early 1770, the failure of the Townshend Acts and success of the nonimportation agreements were evident. Although not all colonies were equally diligent in enforcing the nonimportation agreements and not all goods were banned from import, British merchants nevertheless had lost an estimated £700,000 in trade. Imports of British merchandise into the northern colonies had plummeted a staggering two-thirds. By 1770, the British government had collected the paltry sum of £21,000 since the Acts were instituted.

Once again, the British government succumbed to American resistance and repealed the Townshend duties save only for the tax on tea. It kept the tea tax, Lord North explained, "as a mark of the supremacy of Parliament, and an efficient declaration of their right to govern the colonies."

· 24 ·

Boston Massacre

$\mathcal{I}$n late 1768, as Bostonians were resisting the Townshend taxes and the customs officials dispatched to collect them, four thousand redcoats arrived in Boston. To the colonists, a standing army was considered a further grave threat to their liberties as Englishmen.

The British troops created a poisonous atmosphere in the city. Brawls broke out all over town as armed mobs brought clubs, cutlasses, and shovels to street fights against the bayonet-wielding soldiers. Many on both sides were wounded, and a British lieutenant was slain. A sympathetic local jury acquitted the accused, Michael Corbet. Hostile newspapers and the angry citizenry continued to routinely insult the redcoats.

The British army tried to maintain discipline and punished soldiers who mistreated civilians. It tried to avoid quartering them in people's homes. But, it allowed them to moonlight to earn extra income, causing the Americans to seethe because of the competition for jobs. Moreover, the troops had to defend themselves against mob violence. The city was a powder keg waiting to explode.

The colonists demanded unquestioned allegiance to the patriot cause from their fellow citizens. Violators of the nonimportation agreement were tarred and feathered or hanged in effigy. One merchant, Theophilus Lillie, was labeled an "importer" and thus a traitor to his country. On February 22, 1770, a crowd of hundreds blocked Lillie's shop to prevent him from conducting any business. A neighbor, Ebenezer Richardson, came out of his home to warn off the mob.

The throng pelted Richardson and his house with rocks, sticks, and eggs. One man shouted, "Come out . . . I'll have your heart out, your liver out." Richardson retrieved his musket and stood at a window in the increasingly tense situation. Additional missiles and taunts were hurled. A frightened Richardson fired into the crowd, mortally wounding an eleven-year-old boy in the chest and abdomen. He cried, "I don't care what I've done," as he was seized by the mob, dragged through the streets, beaten, and nearly hanged. Thousands of patriots attended the boy's funeral. Radical Samuel Adams used the young martyr to decry British measures as tyrannical. Tensions in Boston were reaching a boiling point.

On the chilly evening of March 5, a lone sentry, Private Hugh White, was posted by a customs house on King Street. Taunted relentlessly by hostile Bostonians, White smashed his musket into a boy's face. Meanwhile, church bells tolled, signaling a fire alarm and calling more citizens into the streets. The crowd swelled, frightening the sentry. Under a vicious verbal barrage including the words "Damned rascally scoundrel lobster!" White desperately called for help.

Captain Thomas Preston called out a relief party of six privates and a corporal and marched to White's aid. Preston ordered his men to form a line and attempted to disburse the crowd of hundreds. The mob refused, challenged the redcoats to fire, and flung snowballs and ice. Skirmishes broke out along the line. One soldier was knocked down by a club, rose, and fired his weapon. A volley quickly followed, striking eleven Bostonians and killing five. Preston ordered his men to halt their fire and march away from the shocked crowd. Thousands more, bent on vengeance, assembled that night, one man asking, "Can a man be inactive when his countrymen are butchered in the street?" The lieutenant governor, Thomas Hutchinson, attempted to investigate the situation and calm the crowd but was chased off. Preston sounded the alarm for the whole garrison, and further bloodshed was narrowly averted.

Calm was restored when the troops were temporarily removed from the city and the accused soldiers jailed. Both sides rushed to manage public relations, and Paul Revere seemed to have won, publishing his engraving showing bloodthirsty soldiers firing into hapless and innocent civilians. Samuel Adams staged a funeral procession that dwarfed the earlier one. The dead were once again a monument to British oppression.

Samuel Adams's cousin, lawyer and patriot John Adams, boldly defended the British soldiers at their murder trials. Adams wanted to ensure they had a fair trial. It was a courageous stand to take in a city that wanted vengeance more than justice.

Adams adroitly severed the trials of Captain Preston and his men, arguing for Preston that he had delivered no order to fire and in the separate case for the soldiers, Adams argued the opposite, that they were just following orders. Adams exploited the confusion in the conflicting testimony given by witnesses. He even quoted English jurist William Blackstone to defend the killings, telling the jury that "self-defense [is] a law of nature, what every one of us have a right to, and may stand in need of." Captain Preston was acquitted as were most of his soldiers. Two were found guilty though of the lesser charge of manslaughter and punished by a thumb-branding.

One angry radical complained that the trials were "nothing but a mere farce," but John Adams proved that in America, the law was supreme. He staked his own reputation and patriotic credentials on the line to defend rights the colonists themselves were demanding. Within a couple of years, the struggle for rights would lead to outright war.

· 25 ·

Boston Tea Party

$\mathcal{I}$n early 1773, Benjamin Franklin presciently warned from London that "the breach becomes greater and more alarming." That year, Parliament passed the Tea Act to rescue the nearly bankrupt East India Company, whose failure could have had dramatic effects on the British economy. The company was granted a monopoly on the American tea trade and was allowed to send it directly to America to undercut any smugglers. The tea tax of three pence per pound, originally passed with the Townshend Acts in 1767 and retained after most of them were rescinded in 1770, was kept in place.

For the colonists, resistance to the Tea Act was a matter of constitutional principle rather than economic self-interest. "What is it we are contending against? Is it against paying the duty of 3d. per pound on tea because burdensome? No, it is the right only . . . as Englishmen, we could not be deprived of this essential and valuable part of our Constitution," explained George Washington.

Although the resistance to the Tea Act is generally associated with Boston, ships with crates of tea also sailed into the harbors at other ports such as New York, Philadelphia, and Charleston. In each of the cities, local citizens prevented the tea from being landed, threatened tea agents into resigning their commissions, and argued against taxation without representation .

In Boston, at a town meeting in early November, Samuel Adams led the resistance. The meeting adopted resolutions calling on the tea agents to resign, but they resisted. On November 28, the *Dartmouth* arrived in Boston Harbor loaded with 114 crates of tea. Its owner, Francis Rotch, wanted it unloaded.

Some 5,000 citizens crowded around Old South meetinghouse for each of the next two days. The people labeled the tea agents "enemies of the people," posted a large guard around the ship to prevent its being unloaded, and demanded the tea be sent back to England. According to an old statute, the owner of the ship had twenty days to unload its cargo and pay any duties.

In the days to come, two more tea ships, the *Eleanor* and then the *Beaver*, arrived in Boston Harbor and joined the *Dartmouth* berthed at Griffin's Wharf. On December 14, another mass meeting instructed Rotch to seek clearance for a return voyage to England. The beleaguered merchant caved in, but lieutenant governor Thomas Hutchinson refused to clear the ship.

On December 16, one day before the deadline for landing the cargo, 7,000 Bostonians assembled in Old South for a final mass meeting. After one more failed attempt to force Rotch and Hutchinson to send the ship away, Samuel Adams warned the gathering that there was nothing that could be done to save American liberties. The crowd went into a frenzy, crying out, "Boston harbor a tea-pot tonight!" and "The Mohawks are come!"

Thousands of citizens spilled into the streets and marched to Griffin's Wharf on the waterfront. They watched as some fifty men dressed like Mohawk Indians and others with blackened faces boarded the three ships. They hoisted the casks of tea on deck, smashed them open, and methodically dumped their contents into Boston Harbor. The men were careful to do no other damage to the ships. During that wintry evening, they dumped more than 90,000 pounds (45 tons) of tea worth £10,000. "This is the most magnificent movement of all," John Adams rejoiced. "The destruction of the tea is so bold, so daring, so firm, intrepid, and inflexible, and it must have so important consequences, and so lasting, that I can't but consider it an epocha in history."

The British expressed their disdain for the Boston "rabble," but in reality the perpetrators were the town's leaders and honest and sober citizens. The British response was swift and harsh, punishing the province for being a "ringleader" for "seven years in riot and confusion," as it continually violated the British law. Lord North supported punishments to "secure the just dependence of the colonies on the crown of Great Britain."

During the spring of 1774, Parliament passed five acts collectively known as the Coercive Acts. The Boston Port Act closed the harbor to trade until restitution was made for the tea. The Massachusetts Government Act wiped out town meetings and altered the Massachusetts charter and government to place it under greater royal control. The Impartial Administration of Justice Act allowed British officials accused of a capital crime to be tried in England and escape American justice. The Quartering Act permitted the quartering of troops in unoccupied private homes. Finally, the Quebec Act gave Canada the land between the Ohio and Mississippi as well as freedom of religion, raising the frightening specter of a Roman Catholic enemy and "popery" on the frontier. The last was not officially a Coercive Act but the Americans lumped it in with them.

The colonists labeled the new laws "Intolerable Acts," for they seemed to undermine nearly every liberty and right that they held sacred and inviolable. Their economic liberty, their right to govern themselves by their own consent, the right to a trial by jury, the sanctity of their property, their land claims, and their religious liberty were all under assault.

Resistance to the acts unified the Americans in an unprecedented manner. Virginian George Washington thought "the cause of Boston . . . now is and ever will be considered as the cause of America." His fellow members of the House of Burgesses agreed. On May 25, they agreed to a Day of Fasting and Prayer on June 1 in order "to give us one heart and one mind to firmly oppose, by all just and proper means, every injury to *American* rights." The royal governor, Lord Dunmore, dissolved the Burgesses, and they reassembled at Raleigh Tavern where they declared, "An attack, made on one of our sister colonies, to compel submission to arbitrary taxes, is an attack made on all British America, and threatens ruin to the rights of all." They called for nonimportation of British goods and for deputies from the colonies to meet at a general congress.

The people of Massachusetts also called on the other colonies to attend a "meeting of committees from the several colonies on this continent . . . to consult upon the present state of the colonies and the miseries to which they are and must be reduced." They were to deliberate on "wise and proper measures" that would recover "their just rights and liberties, civil and religious, and the restoration of union and harmony between Great Britain and the colonies."

· 26 ·

Continental Congress

$\mathscr{D}$elegates from twelve colonies were chosen by their legislatures and conventions for a national congress tasked with formulating a response to the Coercive Acts. They had a relatively broad mandate. John Adams confided to his diary that the Virginians "appear to be the most spirited and consistent of any."

On September 5, 1774, the Congress assembled at Carpenter's Hall in Philadelphia. Despite the arguments of colonies with large populations, each colony was entitled to only one vote. Congress also resolved to hold secret sessions to encourage free and vigorous debate. The delegates unanimously selected the moderate speaker of the House of Burgesses and president of the Virginia Convention, Peyton Randolph, as its president. Throughout September and October, fifty-six members of Congress debated a declaration of rights, trade restrictions on Great Britain, and a plan for a national government. The representatives deliberated in Congress and negotiated informally in taverns.

On September 16, Paul Revere rode into Philadelphia with the Suffolk Resolves. These militant resolutions came from a county convention and warned forebodingly of "the parricide which points the dagger to our bosoms" and the "military executioners" who thronged the streets. The Suffolk Resolves claimed that the "gross infractions" of the Intolerable Acts violated the rights to which the colonists were "justly entitled by the laws of nature, the British Constitution, and the charter of the province." They asserted that "no obedience is due from this province" to acts designed to "enslave America." Congress endorsed the Suffolk Resolves unanimously and encouraged Bostonians to persevere "in the same firm and temperate conduct" to convince Britain to rescind its "unwise, unjust, and ruinous policy."

One of the first acts of business was a declaration of rights and grievances. Virginian Richard Henry Lee rose and offered that, "The rights are built on a fourfold foundation: on nature, on the British constitution, on charters, and on immemorial usage." Eventually, on October 14, Congress formally approved the Declaration of Rights, proclaiming the "immutable laws of nature" as well as the right to "life, liberty, and property." The colonists had never "ceded to any sovereign power whatever, a right to dispose of either without their consent."

Members of Congress debated the use of trade as a weapon to counter the Intolerable Acts, building on their successful experience of the previous decade. Nonimportation and nonconsumption of British goods and a ban on exports were all considered. Different interests were evident—Massachusetts sought to punish the British for closing Boston Harbor; South Carolina wanted to exempt its rice; Virginia wanted to trade that year's tobacco crop. In the end, compromise was reached and strong trade restrictions were passed.

Congress agreed to nonconsumption of East India Company tea immediately. It voted to ban imports from Great Britain beginning on December 1, 1774, and created a Continental Association to enforce it. Congress deferred to the wishes of the Virginia delegation and passed the nonexportation agreement, which would take effect on September 10, 1775. Applying economic pressure on Great Britain to revoke its taxes had worked repeatedly over the previous decade and there was reason to believe it would succeed again.

Congress expressed its support for republican virtues by resolving to "encourage frugality, economy, and industry" and by discouraging "every species of extravagance and dissipation, especially all horse-racing, and all kinds of gaming, cock-fighting, exhibitions of shows, plays, and other expensive diversions and entertainments."

Congress adjourned on October 26, 1774 and reconvened on May 10, 1775. By then, the first shots had been fired at Lexington and Concord, Massachusetts, and Congress faced decisions about war. In May and June, it voted to secure military supplies and gunpowder. On June 14, Congress approved a plan to raise a Continental Army to support the New England militiamen who had marched to Boston to fight the British.

John Adams nominated Virginian George Washington to command the new army. Washington was chosen for his experience in the French and Indian War as well as for his character. Adams viewed Washington as "a gentleman whose skill and experience as an officer, whose independent fortune, great talents, and excellent universal character would command the approbation of all America and unite the cordial exertions of all the colonies." Washington was a republican general: He promised to defer to the civilian government and refused a salary, asking only that his considerable expenses be reimbursed. He departed for Boston to assume command of the army.

On July 6, Thomas Jefferson and John Dickinson penned the Declaration of the Causes and Necessity of Taking Up Arms. Congress resolved, "The arms we have been compelled by our enemies to assume, we will, in defiance of every hazard, with unabating firmness and perseverance, employ for the preservation of our liberties; being with one mind resolved to die freemen rather than to live as slaves."

Only two days later, Congress approved a final petition to the king for which Dickinson and other conservatives in Congress had pressed. The Olive Branch Petition to Britain promised, "We not only most ardently desire the former harmony between her and these colonies may be restored, but that a concord may be established between them upon so firm a basis as to perpetuate its blessings."

Almost exactly a year later, Congress would declare independence. During the war, it would create a national form of government, ratify treaties, conduct foreign relations, and pay for the war. The Congress was at first an instrument of continental unity and then of American nationhood.

· 27 ·

Give Me Liberty or Give Me Death

*O*n Thursday, March 22, 1775 Patrick Henry was among the delegates to the Virginia Convention at St. John's Church in Richmond. He introduced resolutions, one of which called for raising a militia to defend the colony from the British and to fight the redcoats if necessary. His resolutions set off an animated debate, since moderates preferred to send another petition to England and argue for their constitutional liberties.

Henry rose to speak on behalf of action. As was his custom, he began his speech with a deferential tone and slow pace, gradually building in intensity. He stated that he had a sacred and patriotic duty to his country to speak his mind. Virginia's representatives of the people were shutting their eyes against a painful truth. "Is this the part of wise men engaged in a great and arduous struggle for liberty?" he asked. For his part, he preferred to know the whole truth and prepare for it.

Henry argued that the British were not only oppressing the colonists and rejecting their petitions, but that Great Britain was at war with America. "Are fleets and armies necessary to a work of love and reconciliation?" he asked. Henry believed that compromise was now impossible. He continued:

> Let us not deceive ourselves, sir. These are the implements of war and subjugation—the last arguments to which kings resort. I ask gentlemen, sir, what means this martial array if its purpose be not to force us to submission? Can gentlemen assign any other possible motive for it? Has Great Britain any enemy in this quarter of the world to call for all this accumulation of navies and armies? No, sir, she has none. They are meant for us; they can be meant for no other.

Henry warned that the British plans were nothing less than a conspiracy to enslave them. Many others, such as George Washington, repeatedly described the American condition as slavery. It was more than a metaphor. The revolutionaries believed that they were actually in danger of being enslaved. A free man held property, did not have debt, and was not dependent upon any other man. He governed his own life and his political system. Royal taxes, standing armies, dissolution of representative assemblies—all these threatened American constitutional rights and privileges, and liberty. Henry averred: "They are sent over to bind and rivet upon us those chains which the British ministry have been so long forging."

Henry reiterated that his fellow countrymen cannot keep talking forever. They cannot submit more petitions that would be summarily ignored. They cannot continue to sit supinely as their liberties are stripped away.

> And what have we to oppose them? Shall we try argument? Sir, we have been trying that for the last ten years. Have we anything new to offer upon the subject? Nothing. We have held the subject up in every light of which it is capable, but it has been all in vain. Shall we resort to entreaty and humble supplication? What terms shall we find that have not been already exhausted?

Henry hit his stride. His voice rose and his pace quickened. His audience clung to every word of his rhetoric: "We have *petitioned*—We have *remonstrated*—We have *supplicated*—We have *prostrated* ourselves before the throne—And have *implored* its interposition to arrest the tyrannical hands of the ministry and the parliament."

With another parallel construction, he continued: "*Our* petitions have been slighted; *Our* remonstrances have produced additional violence and insult; *Our* supplications have been disregarded; And *we* have been spurned, with contempt, from the foot of the throne." The conclusion that Henry offered was that, "There is no longer any room for hope."

One spectator, a Baptist minister, noted, "The smothered excitement began more and more to play upon his features and thrill in the tones of his voice. The tendons of his neck stood out white and rigid like

whipcords. His voice rose louder and louder, until the walls of the building, and all within them, seemed to shake and rock in its tremendous
vibrations. Finally, his pale face and glaring eye became terrible to look
upon. Men leaned forward in their seats, with their heads strained forward, their faces pale, and their eyes glaring like the speaker's."

Henry told the assembled representatives and spectators in no
uncertain terms: "We must fight! I repeat, sir, we must fight! An appeal
to arms and to the God of Hosts is all that is left us!" America was in the
right and united in a righteous cause. The principles that the colonists
were fighting for would give them the strength to defeat the great power
of the British Empire.

> Three millions of people armed in the holy cause of liberty, and in such
> a country as that which we possess, are invincible by any force which our
> enemy can send against us. The battle, sir, is not to the strong alone; it is
> to the vigilant, the active, the brave.

To his words, Henry added dramatic gestures. Another spectator,
John Roane, described Henry's gesticulations at the closing of the speech.
Roane said that when Henry mentioned slavery, he made several match-
ing gestures. "He stood in the attitude of a condemned galley slave,
loaded with fetters, awaiting his doom. His form was bowed; his wrists
were crossed; his manacles were almost visible as he stood like the
embodiment of helplessness and agony." Henry stated:

> It is vain, sir, to extenuate the matter. Gentlemen may cry, peace, peace—
> but there is no peace. The war is actually begun! The next gale that
> sweeps from the north will bring to our ears the clash of resounding arms!
> Our brethren are already in the field! Why stand we here idle? What is it
> that gentlemen wish? What would they have? Is life so dear, or peace so
> sweet, as to be purchased at the price of chains and slavery? Forbid it,
> Almighty God!

Henry was saving his greatest line for last. As Henry said these
famous words, he performed his most dramatic gesture. He grabbed an
ivory letter opener and held it high for all to see. He symbolically
plunged the dagger into his breast, shouting: "I know not what course
others may take but, as for me, give me liberty or give me death!"

Henry sank into his chair and let his words sink into his fellow delegates. Henry's words represented the feelings of many American colonists. They would no longer submit to the violations of their liberties with polite petitions. Within a few weeks, America would go to war with Great Britain.

IV

WAR

· 28 ·

Lexington and Concord

$\mathcal{O}$n April 14, 1775, General Thomas Gage received a letter from Lord Dartmouth telling him to "arrest and imprison the principal actors and abettors of the Provincial Congress whose proceedings appear in every light to be acts of treason and rebellion." Dartmouth declared the colony to be in a state of "actual revolt" and instructed Gage that "force should be repelled by force." Gage was "sick of his task" but also believed that the colonists should be dealt with firmly. Gage knew the colonists had military stores at Concord and Worcester. He ordered Lieutenant Colonel Francis Smith to lead ten companies to Concord to seize the stores.

The British did not surprise the Americans in the least. Bostonians watched at least 700 redcoats assembled on Boston Common at ten o'clock on the night of April 18. Villagers in Concord had already heard of the planned British incursion and hid their cache of weapons. While the British waited for supplies and transport, the Americans rang church bells and fired shots to warn of the impending British march. Two riders were dispatched to alert leaders and villagers—William Dawes slipped across Boston Neck on horseback, while Paul Revere rowed first to Charleston and then galloped to Lexington.

Revere warned off John Hancock and Samuel Adams and then rode into Lexington where he met up with Dawes. The pair was joined by a young Dr. Samuel Prescott. After sounding the alarm, the three rode off to Concord, though Revere was captured by a British patrol and roughly handled. Meanwhile, the Lexington militia assembled under Captain John Parker; they then retired to their homes and Buckman's Tavern when the expected enemy column did not appear. Near daybreak, they

97

turned out again to meet an advance guard of six companies of light infantry under Major John Pitcairn.

The British officers commanded the provincials to "lay down your arms, you damned rebels, and disperse." Captain Parker ordered his men to fall out, but they refused to surrender their arms. "Damn you! Why don't you lay down your arms?" the British demanded. A shot rang out. No one was sure who fired the first shot, but the redcoats quickly opened fire and the colonists fired in response. One colonist yelled, "I'll give them the guts of my gun." The British reloaded their muskets and fired another volley. When the smoke cleared, eight Americans lay dead and several were wounded. The rest of the British forces under Colonel Smith joined up with Pitcairn's detachment. The British formed up, gave a victory salute, and marched off to Concord.

Known for assembling quickly, the colonial soldiers were known as minutemen. At Concord, the minutemen had waited on the green since warning bells pealed after midnight. They were reinforced by militiamen from neighboring counties as the word of the British advance spread far and wide. As the sun rose on the horizon, its rays glinted off the arms of the British troops entering the town. One impressed colonist stated, "They made a noble appearance in their red coats and glistening arms." Over one thousand militiamen retreated to the safety of higher ground and waited on British actions.

The British soldiers conducted their warrantless but pinpoint search in the largely deserted town. Six companies were sent to the North Bridge over the Concord River to block the militia and to search farmsteads. In Concord, only a few military stores were found, barrels of flour were dumped out and spoilt, and some gun carriages were burned. A liberty pole was added to the flames, causing a home to catch on fire. Although the flames were quenched with the belated help of British soldiers, the smoke and flame greatly alarmed the militia. One minuteman demanded of his fellow citizen-soldiers: "Will you let them burn the town down?" After a brief war council, the colonists "resolved to march into the middle of town to defend their homes, or die in the attempt."

The American column advanced on the British position. The British fired a volley, dropping several Americans. One colonist yelled, "Fire, fellow soldiers, for God's sake, fire!" The Americans fired into the British position, killing several British officers. After only a few minutes of exchanging fire, the British broke and ran, beating a hasty retreat to the town. The British forces formed up there and began marching back to Boston.

While some militiamen went home, hundreds poured in from distant towns. They advanced through the countryside by horse and foot, outpacing the British column that marched along the road. The colonists concealed themselves behind rock walls, trees, and fences, opening fire on the harried British forces. The militia also set up an ambush at Miriam's Corner. The frustrated redcoats, used to eighteenth-century style warfare involving strict discipline and troop formations, thought the colonists cowardly "rascals" and "villains."

The exhausted British soldiers straggled into Lexington in a disorganized fashion where Brigadier General Lord Hugh Percy had brought up his thousand-man relief brigade. Percy's men trained their artillery on the colonists and inflicted casualties. The British column drove toward Boston, pursued by the relentless militia. The fighting was vicious as groups of men fought hand-to-hand. The Americans continued to assault the British line. The redcoats torched homes to deny the militia cover and refused to give the provincials quarter. The British finally reached Boston as the sun was setting on April 19.

The British suffered an appalling 273 casualties, nearly 20 percent of their forces. The New England militia meanwhile had 93 killed and wounded, less than 5 percent of its men. With "the shot heard round the world," the upstart colonists committed themselves to war with the world's most formidable empire.

· 29 ·

Bunker Hill

$\mathcal{A}$fter the battles of Lexington and Concord, more than 10,000 militia-men swarmed from all over New England to Boston. These citizen-soldiers were led by Artemas Ward, John Thomas, and Israel Putnam. The soldiers often lacked discipline as well as supplies and gunpowder, but they were devoted to American liberty. For their part, the British had three new generals, William Howe, Henry Clinton, and John Burgoyne, who were sent to advise Gage on how to prosecute the war vigorously and end American resistance. Gage and the generals planned to take the undefended Bunker Hill, the highest of the three elevations on Charles-town peninsula, on June 18, 1775.

The Americans learned of Gage's intent, and Ward instructed Pres-cott to march on the hill and build fortifications. On June 16, Prescott and 1,200 men silently moved out in the darkness toward Bunker Hill but actually occupied nearby Breed's Hill. Many of them were farmers experienced in clearing land and used their spades to dig a roughly square redoubt 136 feet on each side with 6-foot high earthenwork walls as par-apets. The British caught wind of American actions when General Clin-ton himself was reconnoitering in the night. Clinton pressed Gage to make immediate preparations for a dawn assault. Gage demurred, giving the Americans precious hours to finish their defenses. At first light, the HMS *Lively* bombarded the American position, but it was already strong enough to resist significant damage. Buildings in Charlestown, however, were struck and the town burned throughout the day.

At a morning council of war, the British generals decided that Howe would make a frontal assault against the entrenched colonists. Although his forces would have to march a quarter-mile uphill, he had disdain for the provincials and expected them to retreat quickly when facing a sizable British force. All morning, while the British slowly prepared for their offensive and stopped for a meal, the weary and hungry Americans strengthened their position. John Stark and his New Hampshire regiment noticed an unprotected left flank at the water's edge and hastily filled the position with a stone and rail fence. Finally, in mid-afternoon, Howe landed some 2,300 men (though no artillery) on the peninsula.

Howe planned to hit the American left flank with his 1,100 men while General Robert Pigot directly assaulted the redoubt with nearly 1,200. Almost 1,500 Americans watched the redcoats march in their line. Both sides were disciplined, waiting until the enemy came within firing distance. When the British approached within fifty yards, the colonists blasted them with a ferocious salvo of musket fire and eight artillery pieces. Many of the British soldiers were killed or wounded, but the survivors were professionals who regrouped to press the attack. Another American barrage smashed the British lines forcing them to fall back.

With their comrades dead or wounded in the tall grass, the British formed up their lines again for another assault. They suffered several casualties at three hundred yards from American artillery. American riflemen hit them with deadly fire at one to two hundred yards. Still the British advanced enemy. The mostly inexperienced and nervous American militiamen wanted to discharge their weapons, but their officers screamed at them to hold their fire. The men were told to aim for where the two shoulder belts crossed on British chests and also to target officers. When the British were a mere twenty-five yards from the redoubt, the Americans fired in a "continual sheet of lightning" and an "uninterrupted peal of thunder" in the words of a British participant. Two hundred British soldiers lay dead while the rest retreated pell-mell. Some devastated companies had only a few men remaining.

Howe was appalled by the unexpectedly slaughter and called on Clinton to send reinforcements of 500 men. The Americans were dangerously low on ammunition, and the British were re-forming their lines. With the reputation of the British Empire at stake, a third wave climbed the hill toward the redoubt. This line suffered the same withering fire from colonial artillery and marksmen. Prescott reputedly yelled to his men, "Do not any of you fire until you can see the whites of their eyes!"

The Americans, most with a single round of ammunition left to shoot, again waited until the British were within range. Men were dropped all along the British line, yet they closed the distance rapidly with their bayonets affixed. Their officers wielded swords against American soldiers who were forced to pick up a cudgel or swing their muskets in fierce hand-to-hand combat, fighting "more like devils than men." The Americans were driven from the field by the onslaught, and many were shot in the back while retreating. Most did escape and crossed the narrow neck to the mainland.

The British won Breed's Hill back from the Americans, but at a dreadful cost. British casualties topped 1,000 men, fully 50 percent of the men. Almost the same percentage of officers who fought that day were also casualties. The British generals reeled at the price of victory. Clinton said it was "a dear bought victory, another such would have ruined us." The colonists suffered nearly 400 casualties.

· 30 ·

Fort Ticonderoga

*O*n the night of May 10, 1775, Lieutenant Jocelyn Feltham, the British commander at Fort Ticonderoga in New York, was awakened by an American force of Vermont's Green Mountain Boys under the command of Ethan Allen and Benedict Arnold. When the irate Feltham demanded to know by what authority Allen was acting, the backwoodsman replied, "In the name of the Great Jehovah and the Continental Congress." The Americans seized the fort, but even though the Continental Army needed the guns during the siege of Boston, Ticonderoga's impressive array of cannon lay idle for six months.

On July 5, a 6-foot, 280-pound Boston bookseller and militia artilleryman named Henry Knox met General George Washington, who had just assumed command of the Continental Army. Knox was only twenty-five years old and impressed by Washington, writing he "fills his place with vast ease and dignity, and dispenses happiness around him." Over the course of the next few months, Washington was frustrated by his inability to break the siege of Boston.

In late October, Knox received a commission from Congress as a lieutenant colonel in the army. Two weeks later, Washington wrote to Congress recommending that Knox command the artillery. While Washington was waiting for an answer, Congress authorized him to procure the cannons at Fort Ticonderoga for use in Cambridge, Massachusetts. Knox volunteered to travel to the fort and retrieve the guns. Washington's generals believed the feat impossible and recommended against diverting precious resources. Washington, however, was struck by Knox's determination. On November 16, Washington told Knox to act with the "utmost dispatch."

Knox and his nineteen-year-old brother, William, rode out from Boston headed for New York City, then pressed up the Hudson Valley. They reached Fort Ticonderoga on December 5. Knox realized that massive sleds were necessary to drag the guns because "the roads are so much gullied that it will be impossible to move a step." He and his brother then took stock of the more than fifty howitzers, mortars, and field pieces, and secured help for moving the sixty tons of equipment. They also recovered much needed barrels of flint and lead balls.

On December 9, they set out on the first leg of their journey. They loaded the massive guns on scows to sail the length of Lake George. Knox went ahead to Fort George to arrange for the sleds and left his brother in charge of the crossing. Strong headwinds impeded the progress and caused one of the scows to founder and sink. The boat was recovered, and the load arrived eight days later. Then, they waited until Christmas Day for the snow to fall.

The convoy pulled through the village of Saratoga and into Albany. It crossed the frozen Hudson River four times without a mishap, though a temporary thaw delayed the journey, forcing it to wait until the river was frozen thickly enough to bear the weight of the guns. Wintry weather returned to upstate New York, and on January 7, 1776, Knox and his men eased the sleds cautiously over the ice. They successfully moved most of them until the ice cracked and an 18-pounder plunged into the river. Incredibly, the men tied ropes to the cannon and used their teams of animals to pull it out. They pushed on toward the Berkshire Mountains.

The men drove their animals up steep and narrow mountain passes through the deep snow. To slow their descent, they had to tie the sleds to trees and put chains under the runners. The progress was painstaking but steady. Knox rode ahead from Springfield on January 24, to report the success of his mission to an elated George Washington. The next day, the artillery arrived to bolster the Continental Army and break the stalemate. It was a remarkable feat, perhaps the war's greatest story of perseverance and ingenuity.

Washington pressed for an attack and, after some initial caution by his council of war, preparations were made to take the high ground at Dorchester Heights, much like the Americans did at Bunker Hill. Since the frozen ground was as "impenetrable as a rock," the Americans had to develop alternative fortifications. Knox launched a diversionary artillery bombardment while the men filled barrels with earth and built timber frames filled with bales of hay. On the night of March 4, 2,000 American troops moved up the hills and began to erect the defenses. Thousands of troops ascended the hill as a relief party. Regiments of riflemen were positioned and the artillery was brought up.

British General William Howe was outraged that the Americans had pulled off the achievement a second time and ordered an attack. Suddenly, a fierce nor'easter slammed into Boston and prevented the attack. The American artillery could bombard British positions and threaten their fleet. Howe grasped the peril of attacking the American position and "judged it most advisable to prepare for the evacuation of the town."

Howe and Washington agreed on terms for almost 9,000 soldiers and 1,000 Tories—Americans loyal to the king—to evacuate unimpeded. The British sailed off for Nova Scotia. Washington marched triumphantly into Boston.

· 31 ·

Common Sense

$\mathcal{I}$n early 1776, war raged across America. The British continued to besiege Boston. The first battles occurred in the South and the port of Norfolk, Virginia, lay in ashes. Yet Americans were still hesitant to make a final rupture with their mother country.

In January 1776, a pamphlet of only forty-six pages fundamentally altered the political debate. Colonists had written pamphlets for over a decade to decry British tyranny, using the cheap and quick print medium to advance their arguments to the public. Pamphlets were read not only by those who purchased them but aloud in taverns, coffeehouses, and public spaces. This gave them a much greater reach than sales figures might indicate. Pamphlets joined newspapers as part of a rich public discourse.

Thomas Paine, a failed corset-maker and tax collector, immigrated to Philadelphia in November 1774. With letters of introduction from Benjamin Franklin, he established himself as a periodical editor. With an eye for universal rights, Paine wrote a newspaper article attacking American slaveowners as hypocrites. "With what consistency, or decency," could the colonists "complain so loudly of attempts to enslave them, while they hold so many hundred thousand in slavery?" he asked. As a result of this piece, he made the acquaintance of Revolutionary physician Benjamin Rush, who suggested that he broach the controversial subject of independence. Paine welcomed this idea. His editors included Rush, Franklin, and Samuel Adams.

Paine wrote in a plain and clear but forceful style that appealed to a mass audience. He originally planned to title the pamphlet *Plain Truth* but yielded to Rush's suggestion of *Common Sense*.

Paine employed ridicule and contempt in his methodical attacks on Great Britain and its tyrannical actions. He called King George III "the royal brute." Hereditary monarchy and aristocracy came under special abuse. Paine called them the "two ancient tyrannies" that were built into the unwritten British constitution. He attacked the idea of monarchy itself, positing that there was no scriptural authority for the institution. Paine denied that nature allowed for the "distinctions of men into KINGS and SUBJECTS." He wondered "how a race of men came into the world so exalted above the rest." Moreover, kings could not be trusted because the "thirst for absolute power is the natural disease of monarchy." Monarchy was, in short, "the most prosperous invention the Devil ever set on foot for the promotion of idolatry."

Paine held hereditary monarchs in particular contempt. No one "by *birth* could have a right to set up his own family in perpetual preference to all others." Some were wise enough to rule but many descendants often proved unworthy of the throne. Paine refused to equivocate: "One of the strongest *natural* proofs of the folly of hereditary right in kings, is, that nature disapproves it, otherwise she would not so frequently turn it into ridicule by giving mankind an *ass for a lion*." The unwise, unjust, and unnatural compact with hereditary monarchs was rooted in fear, superstition, and the plunder of commoners.

Paine countered the arguments of moderates who wanted to reconcile with Great Britain. Colonists had "ten times more to dread from a patched up connection than from independence." Every day, he warned, the last ties between the colonies and Great Britain were breaking. The colonies simply could not "forgive the murders of Great Britain." Reconciliation was nothing but "a fallacious dream."

Paine advocated declaring independence immediately and forming a republican government where "LAW IS KING," rather than vice versa. The colonists had the historic opportunity to form a government according to Enlightenment natural law principles. The purposes of this government were to protect liberty, property, and the free exercise of religion. Paine envisioned representative legislatures sending delegates through frequent elections to a national congress with a president. He wanted to "begin the world anew."

Paine's arguments against monarchy and for republican government were hardly new, as John Adams enviously wrote. Adams called *Common Sense* "a tolerable summary of the arguments which I had been repeating

again and again in Congress for nine months." He may have been correct
but he missed the essential point: *Common Sense* forcefully presented the
various circulating arguments for independence in a single, coherent
pamphlet.

Common Sense went through an incredible twenty-five editions and
sold more than 150,000 copies when America's population was only
three million. Copies were shared or read aloud publicly, expanding its
reach even farther. Few Americans were unaware of this pamphlet.

One Connecticut man attested to the impact of *Common Sense*:
"You have declared the sentiments of millions. Your production may
justly be compared to a land-flood that sweeps all before it. We were
blind, but on reading these enlightening words the scales have fallen from
our eyes." A Massachusetts patriot remarked, "Every sentiment has sunk
into my well prepared heart."

Washington thought that more bellicose acts on the part of British
forces such as the burning of Norfolk only weeks before would provide
stark evidence for Paine's arguments in *Common Sense* and create a popular groundswell for independence. He wrote, "A few more of such flaming arguments as were exhibited at Falmouth and Norfolk, added to the
sound doctrine and unanswerable reasoning contained in the pamphlet
Common Sense, will not leave members [of Congress] at a loss to decide
upon the propriety of separation."

Washington was correct. Within months, movements for independence would gain credence among many of the representatives of the
people in the individual legislatures and the national Continental Congress.

· 32 ·

Declaration of Rights

$\mathcal{I}$n the spring of 1776, several colonies instructed their delegates at the Continental Congress to support a vote for independence, while they also moved toward independence on a more local level as well. Virginians were in the vanguard of the independence movement, both in Philadelphia and at home.

During the previous year, the Virginians chased their royal governor, Lord Dunmore, out of Williamsburg. In August, their representatives met in a Virginia Convention. In November, Dunmore, who some Virginians derided as "our Devil Dunmore" and the "arch traitor to humanity," issued a proclamation declaring martial law and freeing the slaves. On January 1, 1776, Dunmore ordered Norfolk bombarded. The British burned some warehouses, and American soldiers then torched the city, both to deny supplies to the British and to make them appear responsible for destroying Norfolk. Virginians needed no further proof of British intentions.

On May 15, 1776, the fifth Virginia Convention told its delegates to Philadelphia to "be instructed to propose to that respectable body to declare the United Colonies free and independent states, absolved from all allegiance to, or dependence upon, the crown or parliament of Great Britain." It also granted permission for the new nation to enter into foreign alliances and form a national confederation. The citizens of Williamsburg celebrated by firing cannons, holding parades, and pulling down the flag from the cupola of the Capitol.

On the same day, Congress adopted recommendations to the assemblies and conventions of the people in the respective colonies to "adopt such government as shall, in the opinion of the representatives of the people, best conduce to the happiness and safety of their constituents in particular and America in general." John Adams called it "independence itself." This call for colonies to draft their own written constitutions and form their own governments was supplemented by an Adams preamble:

> Whereas it appears absolutely irreconcilable to reason and good conscience for the people of these colonies now to take the oaths and affirmations necessary for the support of any government under the Crown of Great Britain; and it is necessary that the exercise of every kind of authority under the said Crown should be totally suppressed, and all the powers of government exerted under the authority of the people of the colonies, for the preservation of internal peace, virtue, and good order, as well as for the defense of their lives, liberties and properties, against the hostile invasions and cruel depradations of their enemies.

The Virginia Convention followed Congress' exhortation to adopt a new constitution and appointed a committee to draft it and a Declaration of Rights. One was a framework of government. The other was, in the words of Edmund Randolph, "In all the revolutions of time, of human opinion, and of government, a perpetual standard . . . around which the people might rally and by a notorious record be forever admonished to be watchful, firm, and virtuous." Lawyer, patriot, constitutionalist, and representative George Mason was selected to draft it.

Mason began with a stunning statement of natural rights:

> That all men are by nature equally free and independent and have certain inherent rights, of which, when they enter into a state of society, they cannot, by any compact, deprive or divest their posterity; namely, the enjoyment of life and liberty, with the means of acquiring and possessing property, and pursuing and obtaining happiness and safety.

Mason stated that "all power was vested in" the sovereign people and the government was comprised of their representatives and instituted to protect their rights. When it became destructive of those ends, the majority had the "indubitable, inalienable, and indefeasible" right to alter or abolish it. The representatives of the people would be chosen by regular and free elections for nonhereditary positions in a government of separate branches.

The Declaration acted as a Bill of Rights, protecting property; preventing the suspension of laws; protecting criminal rights, trial by jury, and liberty; preventing excessive bail and punishments; banning search and seizures without warrants; and defending freedom of the press as a "great bulwark of liberty." The Declaration protected militias of the people to defend themselves against tyranny and advised that standing armies should be avoided in peacetime. It subordinated military power to the civilian government.

Having affirmed the natural rights and liberties of a free people and proscribed the powers of government, the Declaration noted people's duties to govern their passions, love their fellow men, and worship the Almighty. It also stressed the foundation of republican virtue: "That no free government, or the blessings of liberty, can be preserved to any people, but by a firm adherence to justice, moderation, temperance, frugality, and virtue, and by a frequent recurrence to fundamental principles."

The document stated that religion was the basis of virtue and morality which were in turn necessary for a republican people. As a result of James Madison's efforts, the final document included a statement that "all men are equally entitled to the free exercise of religion."

The Virginia Convention also revised and adopted Mason's draft constitution. The constitution separated the branches of government, created a bicameral legislature, defined the terms for each office, and limited the powers of the executive. In the colony of Virginia, a republican revolution of liberty and self-government had been effected. Delegates to the Continental Congress soon had a copy of Mason's handiwork to guide their own deliberations.

· 33 ·

Declaration of Independence

$\mathcal{T}$he American colonies were at war with Great Britain. The siege of Boston had been lifted, but the British forces were assembling to invade New York. The states were drawing up their own constitutions and declaring their rights. It was time for Congress to confront the question of independence.

On June 7, 1776, Virginian Richard Henry Lee rose on the floor of the Continental Congress to offer the resolution "That these United Colonies are, and of right ought to be, free and independent States, that they are absolved from all allegiance to the British Crown, and that all political connection between them and the State of Great Britain is, and ought to be, totally dissolved."

Lee's resolution sparked a vigorous debate. Delegates John Dickinson, James Wilson, Robert Livingston, and Edward Rutledge protested the measure. They argued that Congress must wait until it heard the "voice of the people." Moreover, the governments of Delaware, Maryland, New Jersey, New York, and Pennsylvania had not authorized their delegates to vote on independence.

Lee, fellow Virginian George Wythe, and John Adams countered that "the people wait for us to lead the way." But Rutledge wrote, "No reason could be assigned for pressing into this measure, but the reason of every madman."

Amid heated passions, Congress appointed a committee of five— John Adams, Benjamin Franklin, Thomas Jefferson, Robert Livingston, and Roger Sherman—to draft a declaration of independence.

The committee met and assigned the task to Adams and Jefferson.

112

In turn, Adams asked the thirty-three-year-old Jefferson to write the document. Jefferson tried to avoid doing it, wishing he was in Williamsburg working on the constitution for the new commonwealth. He had already written a draft constitution but was forced to come to Philadelphia in mid-May. Jefferson wanted Adams to write it. Adams insisted it had to be Jefferson, and he explained why:

> First, that he was a Virginian and I a Massachusettensian. Second, that he was a southern man and I a northern one. Third, that I had been so obnoxious for my early and constant zeal in promoting the measure, that any draft of mine, would undergo a more severe scrutiny and criticism in Congress, than one of his composition. Fourthly and lastly that would be reason enough if there were no other, I had a great opinion of the elegance of his pen and one at all of my own.

Jefferson did not have the advantage of his library while composing the Declaration. But, he readily borrowed from his draft preamble to the Virginia Constitution and George Mason's Declaration of Rights, which was published in the *Pennsylvania Gazette* on June 12. Jefferson was also the author of two key documents arguing for American liberties and rights—his 1774 *Summary View of the Rights of British America* and his 1775 Declaration of the Causes and Necessity of Taking Up Arms. He drew from his knowledge of the works of radical Whig thinkers and the British Enlightenment thinkers such as Francis Hutcheson, Algernon Sidney, and, most of all, John Locke, who had argued for natural rights and self-government in his *Second Treatise on Government*.

Jefferson presented his text to Adams and Franklin who made some edits. On July 1, the Declaration was submitted to Congress and set off a titanic debate between oratorical giants John Dickinson and John Adams. Dickinson carefully reasoned against a hasty separation, earnestly warning his fellow delegates that they were about to "brave the storm in a skiff made of paper." Adams passionately advocated declaring independence. Others joined in the nine-hour debate but a preliminary vote revealed few were swayed and four delegations remained opposed.

No one knows the content of the discussions exchanged that night at the City Tavern and the boardinghouses of Philadelphia, but on July 2, 1776 the members of Congress voted for independence. Opponents John Dickinson and Robert Morris absented themselves, allowing the

Pennsylvania delegation to support independence. The vote of the delegations was unanimous.

Congress revised the document, altering a quarter of the text. An aggrieved Jefferson sat there sullenly. Franklin leaned over and told him a story. A hatter asked his friends for their opinion on a sign that read, "John Thompson, Hatter, Makes and Sells Hats for Ready Money." To his consternation, his friends kept whittling it down, the more they discussed it, until the sign contained only his name and the drawing of a hat.

The final Declaration created a natural rights republic in which rights came from "nature and nature's God," not government. With stirring words, it proclaimed universal principles:

> We hold these truths to be self-evident; that all men are created equal; that they are endowed by their Creator with certain unalienable right; that among these are life, liberty, and the pursuit of happiness.

The document was based on a compact theory of government in which the sovereign people voluntarily agreed to form a republic rooted upon their consent and protecting their natural rights. The people had the right to overthrow a government that failed in its essential duty to protect natural rights.

> That to secure these rights, governments are instituted among men, deriving their just powers from the consent of the governed, that whenever any form of government becomes destructive of these ends, it is the right of the people to alter or to abolish it, and to institute new government, laying its foundation on such principles, and organizing its powers in such form, as to them shall seem most likely to effect their safety and happiness.

A list of grievances indicted the king for "repeated injuries and usurpations" that were proof of a "design to reduce them under absolute despotism." The attempt to impose "an absolute tyranny" justified their severing the bonds of allegiance to the British Crown. "All political connection between them and the state of Great Britain," the Declaration stated, "is and ought to be totally dissolved." With a "firm reliance on the protection of divine Providence," the delegates mutually pledged "our lives, our fortunes, and our sacred honor."

They were treasonous rebels and would be hanged if caught. The Declaration of Independence was adopted on July 4, 1776. It was sent to the printer and fully signed on August 2.

The document was read to American soldiers and the public where it was greeted with great enthusiasm. Bells tolled through the towns and bonfires illuminated the nighttime skies. Thirteen toasts were drunk and thirteen cannons were fired in salute. Citizens processed around Liberty Poles. King George III was burned in effigy.

Americans would have to fight for several long, difficult years before winning their independence, but they had now laid down the foundation for their republic.

· 34 ·

Crossing the Delaware

$\mathcal{T}$he Battle of New York did not go well for the Americans. In the summer of 1776, the British landed 32,000 troops (including 8,000 German mercenaries, generally called Hessians) on hundreds of transport and warships at Staten Island. The invading forces defeated the Americans on Long Island, killing hundreds and taking 1,000 prisoners. The British enjoyed unchallenged naval supremacy and could outflank American positions, forcing the Americans to retreat across the length of Manhattan. General Washington was forced to cross into New Jersey but not before the British captured Fort Washington, bagging more than 100 artillery pieces and almost 3,000 prisoners on November 16.

British Generals Howe and Cornwallis and their army of 10,000 men pursued Washington through the New Jersey countryside. In late November, Washington's army was dwindling. Enlistments were expiring and hundreds of other soldiers simply marched home. On November 29, Washington received 1,000 militiamen from New Jersey but on December 1 he lost 2,000 from that state and Maryland due to their enlistments expiring. Washington reached Trenton on December 2 and implored the haughty Charles Lee to link up his large army but Lee balked. As the British halted at the Raritan River for a few days, Washington crossed the Delaware, taking every boat for miles around to deny them to the British. Still, he feared the river might freeze, allowing the British to cross and threaten Philadelphia. Congress fled in fright, entrusting its general with near dictatorial powers to deal with the crisis. On December 13, Lee was ignominiously captured in a New Jersey tavern by the British. American morale reached its nadir.

The resolve of Washington and his men wavered but did not collapse. Revolutionary financier Robert Morris somehow found supplies for the distressed army. Pamphleteer Thomas Paine, who was traveling with the army, lent his pen to the cause when he wrote *The American Crisis*. Paine appealed to the soldier's patriotism and asked them to endure.

> These are the times that try men's souls. The summer soldier and the sunshine patriot will, in this crisis, shrink from the service of their country; but he that stands it now, deserves the love and thanks of man and woman.

On December 14, the British commanders decided to march back to New York and enter winter quarters. For them, as was common in the eighteenth century, the campaigning season was over. Not for Washington. On December 20, American general John Sullivan arrived at Washington's camp with 2,000 of Lee's men. The enemy forces at Trenton numbered only 1,500 Hessians under Colonel Johann Rall who did not even bother to build defenses around the town. Washington decided a bold stroke would bolster American resolve and end the year with a stunning victory.

On Christmas eve, Washington daringly crossed the Delaware River nine miles above Trenton with an army of 2,400 men. A severe winter nor'easter raged. There were two other forces of 1,500 and 700 men sent across at other points. Artilleryman Henry Knox organized the crossing while the Massachusetts watermen safely ferried thousands of men, fifty horses, and eighteen artillery pieces across the river with a dangerously rapid current and floating chunks of ice. When it landed, Washington's army split into two columns, one commanded by Washington and Nathaniel Greene and the other by John Sullivan. They advanced on the Hessian garrison. The Americans marched through the severe night, many shoeless men with bloody, frozen feet. A few dropped dead from exposure.

The Hessians were not drunk from Christmas celebrations, but they did not expect an attack in such wintry weather and they relaxed their guard. The Americans rushed the town at roughly eight o'clock in the morning. The Hessians were decimated by American artillery on King and Queen Streets, including that commanded by a young Alexander

Hamilton. Sullivan and his men launched a bayonet charge against the Hessian ranks. The Hessians suffered 100 casualties and 900 surrendered while 500 escaped. No Americans were killed in the action and only four were wounded, including Virginian James Monroe. The Americans re-crossed the Delaware, having won a victory they so desperately needed.

Washington's problems were not over. Thousands of enlistments were due to expire on January 1, and he needed another victory to hold his army together. The British learned of the defeat at Trenton, and General Cornwallis marched from New York with 8,000 redcoats. Washington re-crossed the Delaware yet again as arctic temperatures froze the river and allowed Nathaniel Greene's men to walk across. Somehow, Knox ferried thirty or forty pieces of artillery in even more treacherous conditions than Christmas Day.

On December 31, Washington asked his men to stay for one more battle, offering them a hefty ten dollar bounty for six more weeks of service. Some men in New England regiments took the bounty, and Washington mustered other soldiers from Greene's and Sullivan's divisions. A drum roll called for volunteers but no one stepped forward. Washington then appealed to their sense of patriotism:

> My brave fellows, you have done all I asked you to do, and more than could be reasonably expected; but your country is at stake, your wives, your houses, and all that you hold dear. You have worn yourselves out with the fatigues and hardships, but we know not how to spare you. If you will consent to stay one month longer, you will render that service to the cause of liberty, and to your country, which you probably can never do under any other circumstances.

Washington's army swelled to almost 7,000 men. Cornwallis's army marched on Trenton. On January 2, the British column skirmished with the Americans and pushed them back through Trenton to Assunpink Creek, where they stopped the British advance. That evening, the British observed the Americans lighting campfires and heard them making a fair amount of noise in camp. However, it was a ruse—most of Washington's forces marched out into the night toward Princeton.

The Americans covered the ten miles to Princeton by morning, and advance units from the two sides clashed, killing several on both sides. A British bayonet charge sent a panic through the American ranks which retreated. Washington rode up and rallied his troops, helping to turn the tide. "Parade with us, my brave fellows! There is but a handful of the enemy, and we will have them directly," he called to them. The British line broke and the redcoats fled. Washington again encouraged his men: "It's a fine fox chase, my boys!" They drove on to the college where Alexander Hamilton blasted the British garrison with his artillery. With the morning light, Cornwallis discovered that he had been duped and advanced on Princeton. Washington decided that his exhausted men had given all they could and headed to winter quarters in Morristown.

The Battles of Trenton and Princeton were decisive victories, reversing the staggering defeats in New York earlier in 1776. They showed American resolve, both of citizen-soldiers and of their republican general.

· 35 ·

Saratoga

$\mathcal{I}$n the winter of 1776–1777, General John Burgoyne, who enjoyed close relations with George III, persuaded the king to approve an offensive through upstate New York. Burgoyne promised that the rebellion in Massachusetts would be isolated and more easily defeated. Nicknamed "General Swagger" for his bravado, Burgoyne was allowed to attempt a two-pronged assault converging on Albany. With a baffling lack of coordination, General William Howe moved against Washington's army and the capital of Philadelphia. Howe's attack would do little to support Burgoyne's movements to the north.

The American army to the north was hardly more cohesive. New York general Philip Schuyler commanded the northern department but despised the New Englanders under his command as much as they disliked him for his aristocratic and overbearing nature. General Horatio Gates was better liked and lobbied Congress for a command. Congress vacillated between selecting Schuyler and Gates for command of the northern army. Schuyler was in command in early June when Burgoyne's army of 8,300 men and 140 artillery pieces (and a massive baggage train) moved out from Montreal.

Within the month, Burgoyne sailed down Lake Champlain and threatened the decrepit Fort Ticonderoga. American General Arthur St. Clair learned of Burgoyne's movements and quietly abandoned the fort under cover of darkness on July 5. An alarmed George Washington sent a couple of thousand men—including Colonel John Glover and his Marblehead, Massachusetts, men and 800 Green Mountain Boys—swelling Schuyler's army to more than 6,300.

Burgoyne pursued St. Clair but suddenly became lethargic, allow-ing the Americans time to fell trees, alter the path of creeks to flood roads, and destroy bridges. The lengthy British column advanced at a snail's pace. The Americans under Schuyler withdrew to Stillwater on the Hudson, twelve miles below Saratoga. Burgoyne's army ran short on supplies, and he was forced to send out a foraging party under Hessian Lieutenant Colonel Frederick Baum. In mid-August, Brigadier General John Stark ambushed Baum and in savage fighting nearly wiped out the entire expedition, which suffered 900 casualties.

While the fighting was occurring in New York, Congress replaced Schuyler with Gates. The American army almost doubled in size as New England militiamen joined in the fight and Washington dispatched Dan-iel Morgan and his Virginian riflemen north. The army soon numbered more than 11,000. Burgoyne was short on supplies but continued his drive to Albany nonetheless, reaching Saratoga on September 15. Mean-while, Gates moved northward, occupying and fortifying Bemis Heights. On September 19, Burgoyne divided his army into three columns and marched toward the Americans. Benedict Arnold urged Gates to advance and meet the British enemy. Gates equivocated for three hours, then authorized the combined forces of Arnold and Morgan to engage the British. The armies clashed at Freeman's Farm in an epic battle, each side fiercely assaulting the other throughout the day. The Americans with-drew that night, but not before causing more than 560 British casualties. General Clinton marched out from New York, and he might have rein-forced Burgoyne and turned the tide, but he never arrived. Instead, Clin-ton seized a couple of forts along the Hudson River, cut the chain impeding the British Navy, and then returned to the garrison. Burgoyne would not countenance withdrawing. On October 7, Morgan's riflemen moved out and started cutting down the British. Arnold implored Gates to order the army into battle and was relieved of command. Gates sent reinforcements into battle, the Americans taking up position in a forest and laying down a deadly enfilading fire. The insubordinate and brave Arnold disobeyed orders and rushed into battle. He broke the British army, which was forced to retreat, suffering almost 1,000 casualties and the loss of dozens of officers. Arnold was severely wounded, his left femur shattered, but he refused amputation and recovered.

Burgoyne withdrew to Saratoga. Gates pursued him and sur-rounded the British, cutting off any line of escape on October 12. The leaders of the respective armies met on October 16 to discuss terms of surrender, and the following day, the redcoats and their allies marched out and laid down their arms, agreeing to return to England for the duration of the war. Gates had bagged 5,800 prisoners, twenty-seven field pieces, 5,000 small arms, ammunition, and supplies. It was the greatest American victory in the war to date, dwarfing the accomplishments of George Washington.

Congress refused to endorse the terms of surrender and actually altered them. Knowing that the British army would shortly return to America, Congress ordered the prisoners marched to Virginia where they sat out the duration of the war. Soon after the battle, General William Howe resigned. After the British gave up their occupation of Philadelphia the following spring and fought their way back into New York, they would adopt a war strategy focusing on the South.

Perhaps most important, the Battle of Saratoga provided the French with the confidence to sign a treaty of alliance with the Americans and join the war against the British. The American Revolution became a global war.

· 36 ·

French Alliance

$\mathcal{I}$n mid-December 1775, a French visitor, Julien-Alexandre Achard de Bonvouloir, met with the congressional Committee of Secret Correspondence, which had been established to communicate with foreign nations and persons disposed to support the American Revolution. During the secret meetings at Carpenter's Hall in Philadelphia, Bonvouloir claimed to represent the French foreign minister. France was "well-disposed" toward the colonies, he promised, and would consider recognizing American independence and supporting the American war effort.

The committee dispatched former congressional delegate from Connecticut and merchant Silas Deane to establish a relationship with France. Deane was to act as a purchasing agent, securing arms and supplies for 25,000 men. He was also to sound out the French on supporting American independence and trade relations. Even before Deane arrived, King Louis XVI authorized one million *livres* of assistance in the form of munitions to the Americans. The aid would be funneled to the Americans through the fictitious trading company Roderigue Hortalez and Company directed by the author of *The Barber of Seville*, Caron de Beaumarchais. The French foreign minister, Charles Gravier Vergennes, persuaded the king to support America to avenge France's humiliating defeat to Britain during the Seven Years' War. The French were guided more by European politics than by any support for the rights of mankind or for the Americans' struggle for liberty.

While Deane traveled to France and met with Vergennes, America declared independence and became a sovereign nation. Congress selected Benjamin Franklin and Arthur Lee, an American agent in London, to negotiate a treaty of alliance and commerce with France.

The pair arrived in Paris in December 1776. Franklin was a cosmopolitan man of the Enlightenment who was an international celebrity for his scientific discoveries. He was feted by an adoring Parisian population. His face was ubiquitous in the capital, appearing on chinaware, medallions, vases, clocks, and snuffboxes. Franklin quipped that his image was as popular as the moon, and a jealous Louis XVI supposedly stuck it in the bottom of his chamberpot. Dressing as a rustic, backwoods philosopher in his plain clothes and beaver cap, Franklin expertly manipulated his image for diplomatic advantage.

The commissioners' initial meetings with Vergennes were cordial and successful. Although the French initially resisted overtures for an alliance, they did give the Americans another two million *livres* to purchase war material. Until the Americans were victorious on the battlefield and the French navy was better prepared for war, the French were hesitant to formalize any ties with America.

In December 1777, news reached France that British general John Burgoyne had surrendered to the Americans at Saratoga. Simultaneously, the French completed their naval building program and felt ready to go to war with England.

On February 6, 1778, the American commissioners and Vergennes's representative, Conrad-Alexandre Gérard, signed two treaties. The first was a treaty of commerce that provided commercial reciprocity between the two nations. The second was a treaty of alliance in which both agreed to continue the war until America was independent. Neither country would make a separate peace with Great Britain.

In April, Count D'Estaing commanded a fleet of French warships that sailed for America. The fleet also carried Gérard, the first French minister to the United States. When the fleet arrived, it anchored near Philadelphia, and Gérard traveled to the city where he was officially received by Congress. D'Estaing's fleet sailed northward to New York to attempt to help Washington's army assault the British garrison.

When D'Estaing failed to pass the shallows at Sandy Hook, across from New York City, he and Washington agreed to attack the smaller British garrison at Newport, Rhode Island. Generals John Sullivan and Nathaniel Greene, with Marquis de Lafayette, organized the joint attack. A hurricane blasted apart the British and French fleets just as the battle broke out. The British fleet limped into New York, while the French struggled back to Rhode Island to inform the Americans that they were headed to Boston for repairs. Among the passengers in D'Estaing's fleet was Silas Deane, who had been discredited and then recalled by Congress. A radical faction, led by Samuel Adams and Richard Henry Lee, had charged Deane with privately benefiting from his public role. He was also blamed for hiring hundreds of Frenchmen for service in the American army, leading to a number of disputes over rank, when Congress only instructed him to hire a handful of French engineers.

The French Alliance was critically important to the American war effort. The French sent millions of *livres* and essential war material to the fledgling American army. French officers and engineers also lent their experience, such as at the siege at the Battle of Yorktown, Virginia. Major General Marquis de Lafayette served under General Washington in several important battles including Brandywine, Monmouth Courthouse, and Yorktown.

· 37 ·

Valley Forge

$\mathcal{G}$eneral Horatio Gates won a great American victory at Saratoga in late 1777, but General George Washington was much less successful to the south. During that summer and autumn, British general William Howe had sailed from New York and marched on Philadelphia. The American and British forces clashed at two bloody, but ultimately indecisive, battles at Brandywine and Germantown. The British occupied the American capital at Philadelphia, forcing Congress to flee and convene in York, Pennsylvania. Although Congress pressed for an attack to dislodge the British, Washington prudently went into winter quarters after an unimpressive campaigning season.

On December 19, 1777, the bulk of the Continental Army entered the wooded wilderness of Valley Forge, situated in the populous Pennsylvania countryside of dairy and wheat farms. It was a defensible site where the army could train for the renewal of the war in the spring.

Initially the soldiers slept in tents and were divided into work teams to erect wooden huts measuring fourteen by sixteen feet. Prize money was awarded to those who built their huts first. The men were otherwise kept busy constructing redoubts, keeping guard, patrolling, and foraging for supplies. The officers lodged in more spacious and comfortable private homes as was usual.

But the army's supplies were desperately low. Washington immediately appealed to Congress for relief. The army had no meat, little flour, no soap, and few articles of clothing, shoes, or blankets. Washington complained that thousands of men were "barefoot and otherwise naked." He bluntly related his opinion that the consequences of the dire

126

situation were "Starve—dissolve—or disperse." The men in camp complained of their diets of "fire-cakes" (baked flour and water) and chanted, "No meat! No meat!" In late December, the cold and snow compounded their misery and led to cases of frostbite. Meanwhile, typhus and camp fever spread through Valley Forge and thousands were hospitalized.

After the first of the year, the winter was relatively normal and cannot be blamed for the extensive suffering at Valley Forge. Rather, institutional problems and a lack of planning were responsible for a continuing and deadly lack of food and supplies. The Commissary Department was without a general after Thomas Mifflin resigned in October. Congress and Washington had to go to the individuals states to plead for supplies. Some states did comply with the requisitions, but they were suffering their own shortages and keeping supplies for their own troops. The surrounding populace did not want to part with much-needed supplies for worthless Continental money. Washington did not want to commandeer supplies from the population but was eventually forced to send Nathaniel Greene to do so. Even when supplies were available, heavy rains clogged roads and made wagon travel all but impossible.

February was the worst month by far. The starving men were weakened by disease and had no protection against the elements when the temperatures plunged and heavy snows fell. More than 2,500 men—one-seventh of the army—perished during the winter. Hundreds of horses died as well. Gouverneur Morris visited the army that month and was shocked by what he saw: "The skeleton of an army . . . in a naked starving condition, out of health, out of spirits."

Into the picture stepped Baron von Steuben, a German officer with fraudulent credentials who wanted to serve in the American army. Armed with letters of introduction from the American commissioners in France, he traveled to America in late 1777 with a small retinue. He met with Congress, who granted him the rank of captain and accepted his offer to serve without pay. Washington and an honor guard welcomed him to Valley Forge in late February in a relatively perfunctory manner. American officers were suspicious of more foreign officers appointed by Congress and Washington was focused on keeping his men alive.

Washington was, however, open to sound military advice and he listened to Steuben's opinions about a variety of matters. He ordered Steuben to train the army as acting inspector general in early March.

Steuben was a flurry of activity as he labored day and night on a military manual with the help of some translators. He then instituted drills to create an effective eighteenth-century army.

Steuben selected one hundred men to learn the maneuvers as a "model company." Once they were properly trained, they were disbursed to instruct all the brigades. On March 19, a great spectacle commenced. Steuben barked out commands in French, which were translated by Alexander Hamilton and others. The men marched, turned, and wheeled—all without weapons at this point. The Americans, Steuben quickly learned, had an individualist ethos and did not easily defer to authority. He won them over with tempestuous outbursts of anger and spluttered curses in English.

The Americans rapidly felt greater pride and confidence. The Continental Army staged a wonderful show for the observers. More important, the army emerged from a tragic winter a more disciplined and regular fighting force. The abating weather also brought a regular stream of supply wagons into camp.

By June, when the new British commander of the army in Philadelphia, Sir Henry Clinton, decided to abandon the capital and return to New York, the Continental Army had the opportunity to put training into practice on the battlefield. The Americans followed the long British column and eventually attacked at Monmouth Courthouse in New Jersey in blistering heat. Although there were command problems that caused a chaotic retreat and near disaster, Washington rallied his men, who fought with discipline and order.

· 38 ·

Guilford Courthouse

$\mathscr{A}$ s the campaigns in the northern theater of war ground to a stalemate, the British shifted their focus to the South. In May 1780, the British took Charleston, South Carolina, bagging 3,000 American prisoners in the process. After American general Horatio Gates suffered a disastrous loss at Camden, South Carolina, and retreated a humiliating 180 miles in three days, Washington replaced him with Nathaniel Greene. Greene, who was serving as quartermaster general, did not welcome the appointment. He told his wife: "What I have been dreading has come to pass. His Excellency General Washington by order of Congress has appointed me to the command of the Southern Army." But Washington had faith in Greene.

In late 1780, after fruitlessly begging for supplies from Virginia's governor Thomas Jefferson, Greene linked up with his unimpressive army of 800 Continentals and hundreds of militia in North Carolina. Greene broke with military convention and split his forces, giving the boisterous Virginia rifleman, General Daniel Morgan, a command of about 600 men to "give protection to that part of the country and spirit up the people, [and] to annoy the enemy in that quarter." The British responded by splitting their own forces and going after the Americans. Morgan was chased by the feared and brutal British colonel Banastre Tarleton. Greene himself marched out with 1,100 men, pursued by British general Charles Cornwallis. The Americans were greatly outnumbered and undersupplied.

In January 1781, at Cowpens, a cattle pasturing area in South Carolina, Morgan prepared his forces for an assault by Tarleton's army. Morgan created three lines and deployed them based upon their experience and battle readiness. The first line consisted of 150 sharpshooters who were good shots but undependable and bound to break their lines quickly. They were to fire two shots and retreat to the second line, which was also comprised primarily of militia. The job of the second line was to aim for the officers before they then fell back to the third line. The third line, made up of regular troops and Virginia militia, was positioned on high ground. Morgan shored up the morale of his men, crying: "Just hold up your heads, boys, and then when you return to your homes, how the old folks will bless you, and the girls kiss you for your gallant conduct."

When the British advanced, Morgan told his men, "They give us the British halloo, boys—give THEM the Indian halloo, by God!" The plan worked, and the British fled the field, with 100 dead, 200 wounded, and more than 600 captured. The Americans had only 12 dead and 60 wounded.

While Cornwallis was burning his wagon train to increase his mobility, Morgan and Greene reunited their forces. In early February, the Americans decided to move into Virginia, though Morgan, experiencing painful hemorrhoids and rheumatism, resigned and went home. The Americans raced Cornwallis to the Dan River, taking all available boats with them and raising militia in Virginia. Colonel Alexander Hamilton praised Greene's leadership: "To have effected a retreat in the face of so ardent a pursuit . . . [was] a masterpiece of military skill and exertion."

Greene's army of 2,000 would soon double when militia reinforcements from Virginia and North Carolina arrived. They now far outnumbered the British army, even though Cornwallis had also received reinforcements after Cowpens. In late February, Greene re-crossed the Dan. He chose land around the tiny hamlet of Guilford Courthouse to fight.

Greene's battle plan was modeled on Morgan's victory at Cowpens. On the morning of March 15, Greene told his men on the first line, "Three rounds, my boys, and then you may fall back." This time, when the British advanced, the first American line, which consisted of inexperienced North Carolina militia offered feeble resistance and fled, many from the field entirely. The second line, put up a stauncher defense. Finally forced to pull back, the Virginia militia retreated to the third line. The British re-formed their lines and advanced on the Americans in a bloody clash of muskets and grapeshot. The British flanked the American left but were then slaughtered by an American cavalry charge. Nevertheless, the Americans were losing men and had gaping holes in their lines. Greene gave the signal to retreat, and the Americans did so in an orderly fashion.

The British won the field but paid for it dearly with 500 casualties. Greene's army suffered roughly 250 killed and wounded. Greene reported to Congress that, "The battle was long, obstinate, and bloody." The British, he stated, "have met with a defeat in victory." A member of Parliament, Charles James Fox, who opposed the war in America commented: "Another such victory would ruin the British Army."

· 39 ·

Yorktown

*I*n 1780, when the main theater of the Revolutionary War shifted to the South, both sides acted with vigor and achieved victories. As General George Washington guarded the British garrison at New York, forces led by Generals Nathaniel Greene and Daniel Morgan dueled with Cornwallis' army at Cowpens and Guilford Courthouse in the Carolinas.

On May 15, 1781, British general Charles Cornwallis marched into Virginia and reached Petersburg. Cornwallis was reinforced by the American hero-turned-traitor Benedict Arnold, whose 5,000 troops brought the British army up to 7,200 men. Cornwallis received orders from General Henry Clinton to establish a naval station in Virginia and eventually settled on Yorktown. Over the next few weeks, he drove toward Richmond to engage the Continentals under Marquis de Lafayette. Meanwhile, General Banastre Tarleton and his Dragoons pursued Virginia governor Thomas Jefferson, who barely eluded capture in Charlottesville. Cornwallis finally marched his army into Yorktown at the end of July.

Washington had met with the French general, the Count of Rochambeau, back in May to discuss their strategy. Washington pressed for an assault against the British in New York but Rochambeau argued against it. The two continued to bicker over strategy and probe British defenses for weaknesses, though Washington agreed to a possible joint operation in Virginia. Then, in mid-August, French admiral Count de Grasse sent word that he was sailing his fleet from the Caribbean to Virginia but that he could not remain beyond mid-October. Within days, the allies marched toward Virginia.

132

The American and French armies sought to mask their intended destination from Clinton, marching along a route that made it seem as if they were assembling at Sandy Hook, New Jersey, to rendezvous with the French fleet. The seven thousand soldiers, however, marched on, passing through Philadelphia in early September. They sailed down the Chesapeake and reached the James River in Virginia by the middle of the month. Washington separated briefly from his army to visit his beloved Mount Vernon estate for a few days before riding to Williamsburg.

De Grasse arrived in the Chesapeake Bay in late August, landed 3,000 troops, and arranged for transports for the allied armies. He had thirty-six ships of the line and was confronted by an inferior British fleet under Admiral Thomas Graves. The fleets exchanged broadsides and hundreds were killed. The exchange was inconclusive, but it forced Graves back to New York. Simultaneously, Count de Barras, who commanded a separate French squadron, ferried artillery guns from Newport, Rhode Island, to Yorktown.

Cornwallis knew that his position was untenable, writing Clinton, "This place is in no state of defense. If you cannot relieve me very soon, you must be prepared to hear the worst." Cornwallis did not escape allied clutches when he had a chance at Yorktown, and Clinton neither ordered Cornwallis to depart nor sent him reinforcements. Events were moving toward a disaster and the British simply waited for it to happen.

On the other hand, the American and French forces were a model of complex coordination between the two armies as well as between land and sea. Washington met Count de Grasse in a genial exchange and discussed strategy. De Grasse agreed to stay until the end of October. On September 28, the combined armies of nearly 16,000 men formed up in Williamsburg for the short march to Yorktown. They encamped a few miles from the enemy (only 8,000 strong) and began their siege. A contingent of Virginia militia and French marines was sent across the York River to Gloucester to block any avenue of escape. When the allied army arrived, the British abandoned their outer defenses for the relative safety of their redoubts. One American soldier remarked, "We have got [Cornwallis] in a pudding bag."

Washington thought the British "passive beyond conception," but the Americans were extremely active. They took the abandoned Pigeon Quarter and improved its defenses. French engineers then directed the

American sappers to dig a parallel zigzag trench about 500 yards from the British position. On the night of October 5, a stranger appeared to the men and conversed with them. Because it was dark, it was a while before they realized that it was Washington himself. He struck his pickaxe into the earth, commencing the operation and encouraged his men. The British bombarded the American position smartly to impede the construction of the trench, but by October 9, the Americans set up their artillery pieces and responded. Washington ceremoniously lit the match and fired the first gun. The Americans dug a second, closer trench to improve their position and prepared for an assault.

On October 14, Colonel Alexander Hamilton led the American attack on redoubt #10, as his soldiers fixed bayonets and he leaped onto another man's shoulders with his saber slashing. The French swarmed over the defenses of redoubt #9 and suffered heavier casualties. The allied forces successfully took both redoubts and moved up their guns to launch the final assault. On October 16, Cornwallis realized he was defeated and tried to escape across the river, but a severe nor'easter prevented an organized retreat. Cornwallis began negotiating a surrender the following day.

On October 19, the defeated British army and its German allies marched out to stack their weapons. Since an absent Cornwallis pled sickness, Brigadier General Charles O'Hara offered his sword to General Washington. The American refused to accept surrender from a subordinate of Cornwallis and ordered General Benjamin Lincoln to accept it instead. The Americans took 8,000 British prisoners and a few hundred artillery pieces. Lord North reputedly exclaimed, "Oh God! It is all over!" when he heard the news of the British defeat. He correctly surmised that Yorktown spelled defeat for the British. The war dragged on for another two years and included some hard fighting in South Carolina, but the Americans had essentially won the war—and their independence.

· 40 ·

Newburgh Conspiracy

In late 1782, Americans awaited news from France that a preliminary peace treaty had been signed. The Continental Army was encamped at Newburgh, New York, watching the British army that still occupied New York City. American soldiers and officers were disgruntled that they had not been paid in months. On Christmas Eve Congress learned that Virginia had revoked its ratification of a national impost tax, which was a five percent tax on imports. With the tax dead, the government lost a potential revenue source. Nationalists such as Alexander Hamilton, Robert Morris, and Gouverneur Morris, who shared a continental vision and wanted a stronger national government were shocked at the result.

On December 28, a delegation of three officers rode from Newburgh to Philadelphia and conferred with Robert Morris. A few days later, Gouverneur Morris wrote to John Jay, former president of the Continental Congress, "I pledge to you on the present occasion, and although I think it probable that much convulsion will ensue, yet it must terminate in giving to the government that power without which government is but a name." A plan was afoot among the nationalists to use the simmering discontent of the army to force Congress to pass the impost tax and assume greater powers. It was a dangerous game to play in a fledgling republic.

On January 6, 1783, the three officers presented a petition to Congress that was written by General Henry Knox. "We have borne all that men can bear—our property is expended—our private resources are at an end, and our friends are wearied out and disgusted with our incessant applications," the officers at Newburgh complained. In 1780, Congress

135

had promised the officers a half-pay pension for their service in winning independence. The officers wanted to ensure Congress would make good on its pledge as an "honorable and just recompense for several years hard service in which the health and fortunes of the officers have been worn down and exhausted." The officers were willing to accept a lump sum instead of a pension for life, but warned of the dire consequences of not paying the army: "The uneasiness of the soldiers, for want of pay, is great and dangerous; any further experiments on their patience may have fatal effects."

Robert Morris met with Congress, explaining that his office could not pay the army "until certain funds should be previously established." While a committee studied the problem, the officers warned that it could expect "at least a mutiny." Morris ratcheted up the pressure on Congress by tendering his resignation. If Congress did not establish a "permanent provision for public debts," he would leave office.

Despite all the threats, several states adamantly objected to the pensions and the impost tax. Meanwhile, Hamilton tried to win over General George Washington, writing him that "the claims of the army urged with moderation, but with firmness . . . may add weight to the applications of Congress to the several states."

Washington was not taking the bait nor was Henry Knox (despite his initial aid). Knox told the officers, "I consider the reputation of the American Army as one of the most immaculate things on earth. We should even suffer wrongs and injuries to the utmost verge of toleration rather than sully it in the least degree."

The conspirators seemed to have turned desperately to Horatio Gates, the hero of Saratoga, to lead them. Gates was unpredictable, however, and the conspirators feared that he might actually use the affair to overthrow the government. Gates's aide penned an address that stated bluntly: "Faith has its limits, as well as temper; and there are points beyond which neither can be stretched." A meeting of officers was called for March 15—the Ides of March.

Washington caught wind of the plans. He feared that the officers were going to plunge the nation "into a gulf of civil horror." Washington was sympathetic to their plight and the nationalist program but would not countenance military threats to the civilian government. When their meeting convened, Washington unexpectedly marched into the newly-built meetinghouse, appropriately called the Temple of Virtue, to address his men. He told them he had shared their privations during the war and their current frustrations. But he asked them not to tarnish their shining military achievement. Finally, he appealed to their patriotism and republican principles:

> Let me conjure you, in the name of our common country, as you value your own sacred honor, as you respect the rights of humanity, and as you regard the military and national character of America, to express your utmost horror and detestation of the man who wishes, under any specious pretences, to overturn the liberties of our country, and who wickedly attempts to open the flood gates of civil discord, and deluge our rising empire in blood. . . . By thus acting you will give one more distinguished proof of unexampled patriotism and patient virtue, rising superior to the pressure of the most complicated sufferings. And you will, by the dignity of your conduct, afford occasion for posterity to say, when speaking of the glorious example you have exhibited to mankind, "had this day been wanting, the world had never seen the last stage of perfection to which human nature is capable of attaining."

Washington loved the theater throughout his life, especially his favorite play, Joseph Addison's *Cato*. He had a flair for the dramatic gesture. He pulled out a pair of spectacles, candidly admitting his declining vigor in front of his men while muttering, "Gentlemen, you will permit me to put on my spectacles, for I have not only grown gray, but almost blind, in the service of my country."

The cabal collapsed on the spot. The tension broke and the officers wept openly. They pledged their "unshaken confidence" in Congress.

Congress eventually voted for an impost tax and an army pension but it was so watered down that even Hamilton voted against it, and ultimately the states refused to ratify it. In the end, Congress's inability to raise money led many to believe a new constitution was needed. But for now, Washington's principled actions had preserved Congress, republican government, and American liberties.

· 41 ·

Peace Treaty of 1783

$\mathcal{O}$n June 15, 1781, Congress voted to appoint a commission of five—John Adams, Benjamin Franklin, John Jay, Thomas Jefferson, and Henry Laurens—to negotiate a peace treaty with Great Britain and to secure independence. Congress drafted instructions to the commissioners with a controversial clause ordering them not to act without consulting the French government: "Undertake nothing in the negotiations for peace or truce without their knowledge and concurrence; and ultimately to govern yourselves by their advice and opinion, endeavoring in your whole conduct to make them sensible how much we rely upon his majesty's influence for effectual aid in everything." Opponents complained privately that, "Our allies are to rule the roost."

The American victory at Yorktown devastated British morale at home and led to the fall of Lord North's ministry; he resigned in March 1782. The Marquis of Rockingham replaced North and led a divided ministry. The king bowed to the reality that the British could not defeat the colonies militarily and would have to end the war. However, the British were also unwilling to grant America independence in the peace treaty and fought it tooth and nail.

For a while, Franklin was the only negotiator. Jefferson never left for Paris, Laurens was captured at sea by the British and imprisoned in the Tower of London, Adams was in the Netherlands securing a loan, and Jay didn't arrive until June 1782. Franklin was a shrewd and subtle diplomat, carrying on relatively secret negotiations with the Scottish merchant Richard Oswald without offending the French. He was also uncompromising in his demands for American independence.

On July 1, Rockingham suddenly died and was replaced by Lord Shelburne. By July 10, Franklin submitted his plan to Oswald dividing peace negotiations into necessary and advisable articles. The first and most necessary article was "independence full and complete in every sense, to the thirteen states." Franklin also included boundaries with Canada and American fishing rights off Newfoundland. The advisable articles included indemnifying "many people who had been ruined by towns burned and destroyed," admitting British war guilt, granting America access and free trade in British ports, and ceding Canada to America as well. Shelburne was interested in making peace so that he could dispatch troops to fight the French in the West Indies. Consequently, he allowed Oswald to proceed with negotiating on the basis of Franklin's necessary articles, though he instructed Oswald to separate America from its French ally.

In August, Jay had recovered well enough from his bout with influenza to negotiate alongside Franklin. He distrusted both French and British diplomats, and took a hard-line approach. He was irate that Oswald's commission instructed the Scot to negotiate with the American colonies rather than a sovereign nation. Jay finally persuaded the British to call his country the United States of America. Jay also pushed hard to win territory to the Mississippi River and navigation rights. The French balked at this. Their support for America was based on a desire to strike a blow against Britain, not to create an American empire. Vergennes tried to get the Americans to tone down their territorial demands. Jay was outraged and supposedly had an exchange with Franklin when he yelled that he would break Congress's instructions not to act without the consent of the French. "If the instructions conflict with America's honor and dignity I would break them—like this!" and smashed his clay pipe into a fireplace.

Franklin was laid low by a debilitating kidney stone in late August and early September, allowing Jay to seize control of the negotiations. Jay distanced himself from the French and more or less proceeded without them. Jay drafted a treaty (based largely on Franklin's plan), and the British largely accepted the necessary articles though they pushed back on the fishing rights and demanded Americans pay pre-war debts to British merchants and compensate Tories for their confiscated property.

Franklin reentered the negotiations in late September, and the American team was bolstered by the arrival of John Adams on October

26. When the British adamantly demanded compensation for the Tories, Franklin angrily retorted that the British were to pay reparations for the burning of Charlestown (near Boston), Norfolk, Falmouth, and New London. He reminded Oswald, "You will please recollect, that you have *not* conquered us."

On November 29, Henry Laurens arrived to join the commissioners while Adams thundered about the fishing rights: "Gentlemen, is there or can there be a clearer right? . . . When God Almighty made the Banks of Newfoundland at three hundred leagues distance from the people of America and six hundred leagues distance from those of France and England, did he not give as good a right to the former as to the latter?"

On November 30, both sides signed the preliminary peace treaty, granting America its independence as well as Newfoundland fishing rights and navigation rights on the Mississippi. The Americans conceded that Tories should receive restitution and pre-war debts should be paid, though without any real expectation that either would happen. The British also promised to evacuate their forts in the American West, but they too reneged. The participants held a dinner at Franklin's country estate, Passy, and managed a few final jabs at each other.

A few days later, Franklin met with a displeased Count de Vergennes, who had been excluded from the talks despite Congress's instructions. Franklin offered his apologies and had the audacity then to ask for a loan of six million *livres*. Despite the tensions, Vergennes agreed to the loan. The money was sent with the preliminary peace treaty to Congress on board the ship *Washington*.

Congress assented to the terms of the treaty, and Franklin, Adams, and Jay signed the final treaty on September 3, 1783. Congress ratified it the following winter. America was an independent nation.

· 42 ·

Washington Surrenders His Commission

$\mathcal{O}$n March 12, 1783, Congress officially received notice that its commissioners had signed a peace treaty with the British. As a result Washington furloughed most of his soldiers who simply retired to their homes. In June, some soldiers from the Pennsylvania line, frustrated at not being paid, mutinied. They chased Congress out of Philadelphia, and then made their way to Trenton and then Annapolis. It was not a glorious demobilization of the men who fought for their country's independence.

In his final few months of command, General George Washington announced his intention to retire and offered his thoughts about the shape of the new republican nation. In his Circular Letter of June 14, addressed to the states, Washington explained that the most important pillar of independence and liberty was "an indissoluble Union of the states under one federal head." Besides a strong national government, Washington wished for citizens to cultivate a "brotherly affection and love for one another, for their fellow citizens of the United States at large."

After eight years of commanding the army, Washington yearned for his home and family. He paraphrased the Book of Micah to several correspondents: "It being my anxious desire to quit the walks of public life, and under the shadow of my own vine, and my own fig-tree, to seek those enjoyments, and that relaxation, which a mind that has been constantly upon the stretch for more than eight years, stands so much in need of."

On November 2, he thanked his men for their service in the army. They fought with many disadvantages and deprivations, yet they endured

141

and won a victory over a formidable power against great odds. "The singular interposition of Providence . . . [and] the unparalleled perseverance of the armies of the United States, through almost every possible suffering and discouragement for the space of eight long years, was little short of a standing miracle." He again described the idea of a Union and national character, impressed that "men who came from the different parts of the continent . . . would instantly become but one patriotic band of brothers."

Later that month, Washington marched with a small group of soldiers into New York, which the British had occupied since 1776 and from which they had agreed to depart when the final peace treaty arrived. At Fraunces Tavern, Washington said a tearful farewell to several of his officers including Henry Knox and Baron von Steuben. Washington expressed his gratitude for their service and wished them well. Overcome with emotion, he simply invited them to come forward: "I cannot come to each of you but shall feel obliged if each of you will come and take me by the hand."

Washington was feted by citizens and public officials as he proceeded to Congress in Annapolis. He was saluted, toasted, and honored with dinners and balls. Finally, on December 23, Washington appeared before Congress to surrender his military commission. He said:

> Happy in the confirmation of our independence and sovereignty, and pleased with the opportunity afforded the United States of becoming a respectable nation, I resign with satisfaction the appointment I accepted with diffidence. . . . The successful termination of the war has verified the most sanguine expectations, and my gratitude for the interposition of Providence, and the assistance I have received from my countrymen. . . . Having now finished the work assigned me, I retire from the great theater of action; and bidding an affectionate farewell to this august body under whose orders I have so long acted, I here offer my commission, and take my leave of all the employments of public life.

Washington withdrew from his pocket the withered parchment containing his original commission from 1775. He stepped forward and handed it solemnly to President Thomas Mifflin. Everyone in the hall was wiping tears from their eyes.

Washington's resignation confirmed that in the American republic, the military was subordinate to the civilian government. His actions were compared to those of the legendary Roman general Cincinnatus, who served his country in its war for independence and then returned to his plow. King George III reportedly said, if Washington voluntarily surrendered power, he "will be the greatest man in the world."

V

NATIONHOOD

· 43 ·

Virginia Statute for Religious Freedom

$\mathscr{B}$ack in June 1776, George Mason penned the Virginia Declaration of Rights. It declared natural rights and proclaimed essential liberties. When writing about religious liberties, Mason, influenced by the ideas of John Locke's *Letter Concerning Toleration*, wrote, "All men should enjoy the fullest toleration in the exercise of religion according to the dictates of conscience." A young James Madison offered an amendment that fundamentally altered the liberal principle of toleration to a new and revolutionary one—religious liberty. The Declaration of Rights read: "All men are equally entitled to the free exercise of religion, according to the dictates of conscience."

Madison's fellow delegates accepted that freedom of religion was an inalienable right (and a duty to God), but they were unwilling to accept Madison's amendment that effectively disestablished the official Anglican Church. Petitions soon flooded the House of Delegates from Baptists, Presbyterians, and Lutherans calling for disestablishment. The legislature responded to the demands of their constituents, relieving dissenters of paying taxes for the support of the Anglican Church.

In early 1777, Thomas Jefferson joined the cause of religious liberty. As an Enlightenment thinker, Jefferson believed that religion was a matter of reason and equated religious liberty with freedom of thought. The resulting Bill for Establishing Religious Freedom was debated in the General Assembly in 1779. Jefferson opened the bill with a lengthy preamble: "Well aware that the opinions and belief of men depend not on their own will, but follow involuntarily the evidence proposed in their minds; that Almighty God hath created the mind free," and thus was free

147

from restraint by civil government. Jefferson affirmed that, "The opinions of men are not the object of civil government." The bill would enact disestablishment as "no man shall be compelled to frequent or support any religious worship, place, or ministry whatsoever, nor shall be enforced, restrained, molested, or burdened in his body or goods, nor shall otherwise suffer, on account of his religious opinions or belief."

The bill was soundly defeated. Also in 1779, the General Assembly began considering a general assessment of nondiscriminatory taxes to support various religious denominations. The idea of taxes to support churches coexisted with religious liberty in the minds of many during the Revolutionary generation. They argued that republican government depended on the virtue of its citizenry and leaders, and that virtue was in turn rooted in religion. One petition sent to the legislature in Virginia noted:

> True religion is most friendly to social and political happiness. That a conscientious regard to the approbation of Almighty God lays the most effectual restraint on the vicious passions of mankind, affords the most powerful incentive to the faithful discharge of every sacred duty and is consequently the most solid basis of private and public virtue is a truth which has in some measure been acknowledged at every period of time and in every corner of the world. It is a truth sanctioned by the reason and experience of the ages.

In 1784 there was a groundswell of support for a general assessment. The tax money could be allocated to the denomination of the person's choice (to pay for clergy or a "mode of worship") or to schools and education rather than religion. It did not establish a particular denomination or even Christianity broadly as the state religion, but rather sought to support religion to inculcate virtue for republican government.

The supporters of the bill included an impressive array of Virginia statesmen and the public. Patrick Henry, a leading proponent, was joined by Richard Henry Lee, John Marshall, Edmund Pendleton, and George Washington, among others. On the other side, Baptists, Methodists, Quakers, and after some wavering, Presbyterians (who opposed the bill because of the persecution they faced under the Anglican Church), formed an improbable alliance with Madison and Jefferson (neither of whom was especially known for his piety). On November 11, 1784, the House of Delegates passed the resolution for a general assessment by a vote of forty-seven to thirty-two. Henry was appointed to chair a committee to draft a bill on the subject. Then, he was abruptly removed from the debate when the Assembly chose Henry governor.

The bill's opponents in the Assembly thereby gained momentum and the religious dissenters bolstered the cause with their own petitions. The tide turned against the assessment and in favor of disestablishment. One of the anonymous writers who issued a pamphlet to defeat the assessment was James Madison. He believed that the assessments were an assault on religious freedom. In his "Memorial and Remonstrance Against Religious Assessments," Madison wrote: "The religion then of every man must be left to the conviction and conscience of every man; and it is the right of every man to exercise it as these may dictate. This right is in its nature an unalienable right."

The Virginia Statute for Religious Freedom passed into law on January 16, 1786. The Assembly enacted the idea into law that:

> No man shall be compelled to frequent or support any religious worship, place, or ministry whatsoever, nor shall be enforced, restrained, molested, or burthened in his body or goods, nor shall otherwise be made to suffer, on account of his religious opinions or belief. . . . We are free to declare, and do declare, that the rights hereby asserted are of the natural rights of mankind.

Most states pursued religious liberty as a fundamental right and disestablished their churches, though not all did. In the 1830s, Massachusetts became the last state to disestablish. The American Revolution won both civil and religious liberty for the American people.

· 44 ·

Annapolis Convention

$\mathcal{A}$fter the Peace Treaty of 1783, the new United States was an independent nation but not a harmonious one. The Articles of Confederation, which the states ratified in 1781, allowed the states to regulate commerce. Several states engaged in trade wars with one another which almost descended into actual shooting wars.

Maryland and Virginia disputed control of the lucrative navigation of the Potomac River. Commissioners from both states met at George Washington's plantation, Mount Vernon. On March 28, 1785, they signed an agreement to cooperate on the Potomac. More important, the Mount Vernon Conference resulted in Virginia's John Tyler proposing in the Virginia legislature that the state call on all the states to send delegates to a conference to discuss "the requisite augmentation of the power of Congress over trade." Enough states agreed and the convention was set for the first Monday in September, 1786 in Annapolis.

James Madison prepared for the convention by studying history and political theory for months, and producing a lengthy study of "Ancient and Modern Confederacies." The work examined the deficiencies of the Articles of Confederation. A potential ally in New York, Alexander Hamilton, had for several years supported the idea of a convention to revise the Articles and managed to get himself elected as a commissioner to the Convention. Hamilton's hopes for the Annapolis Convention went beyond merely a uniform system of commercial regulations. George Washington privately noted that, "A general convention is talked of by many for the purpose of revising and correcting the defects of the federal government."

The senate of the host state Maryland announced in March that it would not send delegates out of fear that it might "produce other meetings, which may have consequences which cannot be foreseen." Other states—Connecticut, Georgia, and South Carolina—also refused to participate, showing how much opposition there was to strengthening the powers of the general government. Madison arrived in Annapolis on September 4, and stayed at Mann's Tavern, the site of Washington's 1783 retirement dinner. Hamilton joined Madison and a few commissioners from New Jersey a few days later. On Friday, September 8, as they waited for the other commissioners to arrive for a quorum, Madison glumly wrote his brother: "The prospect of a sufficient number to make the meeting respectable is not flattering." By the end of the weekend, only twelve commissioners from five states had reached the city, and only three of those had enough representatives to vote formally at the meeting.

With bleak prospects of achieving anything substantive, the commissioners began meeting on Monday, September 11. They elected John Dickinson of Delaware as chairman. Frustrated that they could not make decisions with so few states represented, they appointed Edmund Randolph to draw up a report for the states. While there is no extant record of the proceedings or the informal discussions among the commissioners, it is evident that a consensus developed that more radical nationalist reform was necessary. Madison wrote that each delegate was "being fortified in his sentiments and expectations by those of others." Pennsylvania's Tench Coxe wrote that, "Since my journey to Annapolis . . . I have deemed capital alterations in our general government indispensably necessary."

Hamilton, who was desperate to enhance the powers of the national government, wrestled responsibility for composing the report from Randolph. Hamilton's first draft was too extreme even for the nationalists at the convention. Madison advised Hamilton to tone down his language and submit to alterations, especially those suggested by Randolph. "You had better yield to this man, for otherwise all Virginia will be against you," Madison told the New Yorker.

The final report, approved unanimously by the commissioners on September 14, was radical enough. "That there are important defects in the system of the federal government is acknowledged by the acts of all those states, which have concurred in the present meeting," it began.

Those defects were "greater and more numerous" than previously admitted and led to the "embarrassments which characterize the present state of our national affairs." They reasoned that the problems merited a "deliberate and candid discussion" to explore possible solutions. Therefore, the commissioners made the bold call for the states to:

> Meet at Philadelphia on the second Monday in May next, to take into consideration the situation of the United States, to devise such further provisions as shall appear to them necessary to render the constitution of the federal government adequate to the exigencies of the Union and to report such an act for that purpose to the United States in Congress assembled.

With that, the convention concluded and the delegates departed for their respective states. By then, the Massachusetts and Rhode Island delegates were on their way, and Hugh Williamson was delayed while traveling from North Carolina.

It is unknown whether the commissioners were rushing to finish their task before any dissenting opinions could be voiced from others who were coming. They may have simply proceeded in their work, despairing of any other favorable outcome to resolving commercial disputes. The national Congress would have to decide whether to follow its recommendations to call a convention to consider revising the Articles of Confederation.

· 45 ·

Shays' Rebellion

$\mathcal{I}$ndependence did not bring prosperity to many parts of the United States. Britain restricted American trade with the West Indies, which was a critical part of the pre-war trade routes between Europe, Africa, and the Americas and the Caribbean. Exports slumped while imports of British goods resulted in a shortage of specie. Paper money was virtually worthless because of inflation. Meanwhile, taxes (especially on land) were increasing in order to pay off the Revolutionary War debts.

New England in particular was in the throes of a postwar economic depression. Farmers in western Massachusetts suffered greatly from a credit crunch when their debts to eastern merchants and shopkeepers were called in. When they were unable to pay the debts except in crops, they were sued in local courts. These proud and independent yeoman farmers lost their farms, ended up in debtors' prisons, and paid higher taxes than wealthy elites.

In the summer of 1786, farmers in the western counties met in conventions of the people, assembling peacefully to write petitions to the Massachusetts General Court. They asked for a fairer tax system, relief from debts through a tender (barter) system, an inflationary paper currency, a capital relocated away from the commercial interests in Boston, and, most important, the abolition of the debtor courts. The eastern elites defended their own interests and the sanctity of property and contracts. The merchants even encouraged the farmers to live more frugally and virtuously. "Industry, economy, and honest principles, with the aid of a little patience and performance," noted one merchant, would solve their economic woes. Others disdainfully told the farmers to stop drinking so much and buying so many luxuries.

Since the eastern elites had summarily ignored their plight, the irate farmers recalled the popular and violent resistance to tyranny of the 1760s. One farmer argued that the eastern interests were attempting to "drive out that hardy and independent spirit from among us, and forge the chains for our liberties so strong, that the great exertions and convulsions will not break them." Beginning in late August, the farmers converged on the county courts to shut down these symbols and engines of their oppression. If the courts could not meet, they reasoned, the farmers could not be sued for debts or lose their land. They held meetings in local taverns and plotted their strategy.

On August 29, 1,500 armed and angry farmers marched on the Northampton courthouse and closed it. On September 5, the court tried to meet in Worcester, but 300 bayonet-wielding farmers blocked access to the important officials they heckled. The rebels proceeded to shut down courts in Middlesex, Plymouth, and Berkshire Counties over the next month; the Massachusetts Supreme Court was also prevented from meeting in Springfield by a crowd of 1,500 in late September. Governor James Bowdoin was outraged. He attempted to call out the militia, but many of its members refused to march against their neighbors and kinfolk, and some joined the rebels.

The response of the state and national government was swift and severe. The Continental Congress resolved to raise 1,340 troops, but there was little money and few recruits forthcoming from the states. The General Court convened and passed several draconian laws to deal with the crisis. On October 24, the Militia Act made it a crime to join with "any mutiny or sedition." The crime was punishable by court-martial. Four days later, the Riot Act prohibited twelve or more armed persons from assembling and empowered sheriffs to kill rioters. Rioters could also lose their lands, suffer a whipping with thirty-nine lashes, and be jailed. On November 10, the writ of habeas corpus was suspended, authorizing the roundup of suspected traitors. The government did offer a pardon to draw rebels off the movement but few stepped forward to accept.

The courts were closed or recessed during October, and many of the farmers returned home to harvest their crops. Another round of troubles began in November and December when courts in Worcester and Springfield tried to re-open and were again forcibly closed. On January 4, 1787, with no national army forthcoming, Governor Bowdoin decided to raise a private subscription army of 4,400 soldiers without legislative approval. As many as 150 wealthy individuals from the eastern counties contributed funds to support the army under the leadership of Revolutionary War general Benjamin Lincoln. It was to secure "system and order" in the western Massachusetts countryside.

The rebellious farmers organized under the leadership of Daniel Shays, a captain during the Revolution, and others. Their leaders called on them to "immediately assemble in arms to support and maintain not only their rights, but the lives and liberties of the people." Ominously, they announced their intention to smash the "tyrannical government in Massachusetts." They were guided by Revolutionary republican principle that they had every right to overthrow a tyrannical government and replace it with one of their choosing. The Shaysites planned an assault against the federal arsenal at Springfield, which housed thousands of muskets, barrels of gunpowder, shot, and other military stores. About 1,200 militiamen awaited the attack; Lincoln's large army was defending the Worcester court.

The rebel army of almost 2,000 men approached Springfield and was divided into three regiments. The leaders planned a three-pronged assault on January 25 but then postponed the attack for one day. The letters informing the regiments of the delay were intercepted, and two of the regiments proceeded with the attack as scheduled. On January 25, 1,500 Shaysites advanced on the arsenal slowly, trudging through four-foot snow drifts and urged on by Shays. The defending militia fired warning shots from their cannon over the heads of the insurgents, "humanely wishing to frighten them to lay down their arms." When the farmers kept coming, the militia fired grapeshot, which left four dead and twenty others wounded. The farmers retreated. The battle for the arsenal was over.

Other skirmishes were fought, but the rebellion was largely ended. On February 4, the General Court declared a state of "open, unnatural, unprovoked, and wicked rebellion," granting the governor the power to declare martial law and raise additional troops. Shays and other leaders fled to Vermont and New York to escape prosecution, though thirteen Shaysites were rounded up, tried, and sentenced to death. The governor wisely pardoned them.

Shays' Rebellion had dramatic effects on the minds of those nationalists who wanted to strengthen the national government. James Madison believed that the insurrection gave "new proofs of the necessity of such a vigor in the general government as will be able to restore health to any diseased part of the Federal Constitution." The crisis seemed stark evidence of the weakness of the central government and provoked support for the Philadelphia Convention meeting in May 1787. Washington, who received exaggerated dire warnings from his friend, Henry Knox, stated: "They exhibit a melancholy proof of what our transatlantic foe have predicted . . . that mankind, left to themselves are unfit for their own government. I am mortified beyond expression when I view the clouds which have spread over the brightest morn that ever dawned upon any country."

· 46 ·

Constitutional Convention

$\mathcal{T}$he delegates who attended the Constitutional Convention were highly-educated and public-spirited statesmen. They were experienced in the Revolutionary War and national and state politics: eight had signed the Declaration of Independence, fifteen had helped draft state constitutions, twenty-one had fought in the Revolutionary War, and three-quarters had been members of the Continental Congress. The majority were lawyers but there were also merchants and planters. They were, in the words of John Adams, men of "ability, weight, and experience" (even though John Adams, Samuel Adams, John Hancock, Patrick Henry, Thomas Jefferson, and Richard Henry Lee were not present).

One indispensable delegate was the revered hero of the American Revolution, George Washington, who was an ardent nationalist and deeply concerned about the fate of the fledgling country. Although he was committed to strengthening the national government, Washington struggled over whether to attend the Philadelphia Convention. He had publicly retired and was alarmed that he might be perceived as a Caesar attempting to seize the reins of power. Perhaps he also feared what would happen to his reputation if the government should fail while he stood idle, or conversely, if it succeeded without his participation. In the end, he chose to attend, and although he spoke little, his very presence gave legitimacy to the endeavor.

Another important figure was Princeton graduate and Virginia congressman James Madison. The brilliant Madison again turned to history to help him prepare for the Convention. He composed an essay, "Vices of the Political System," enumerating the problems of the Articles of

Confederation and proposing remedies. When he and Washington arrived in Philadelphia in early May 1787, they had several days to meet with the rest of the Virginia delegation, as well as the Pennsylvania delegation, to draft a plan that would dominate the discussion of the framework of government for the duration of the summer.

On Friday, May 25, the delegates assembled in the Pennsylvania statehouse. Unsurprisingly, they unanimously voted for Washington to preside over the convention. A rules committee was appointed and chaired by the inestimable legal mind from Virginia, George Wythe. The following Monday, the delegates agreed that their discussions would be held according to rules of civility and decorum. They also decided that each state delegation would have only one vote. And they agreed that they would conduct their business in secret, thus allowing for greater candor and free and open debate.

On Tuesday, May 29, Virginian Edmund Randolph rose and introduced the fifteen resolutions that comprised the Virginia Plan. It would create a bicameral Congress based upon proportional representation in two houses, an independent executive, and a national judiciary. Significantly, the plan would give the national government a veto over state laws. Finally, it proposed to send the final work of the convention to popular ratifying conventions in the states rather than the legislatures.

The intent of the Virginia Plan was evident—to strengthen the power of the national government. The next day, Charles Pinckney of South Carolina demanded to know whether Randolph "meant to abolish the state governments altogether." Because of the experience under the weak government of the Articles of Confederation, James Madison thought that a stronger government would best "provide for the safety, liberty, and happiness" of the people. George Read of Delaware threatened to walk out of the convention (the first of many delegates to do so) because his small state instructed him not to accept any plan that did not give equal weight to the states in the national legislature. Charles Cotesworth Pinckney of South Carolina raised the fundamental objection that the convention was exceeding its mandate by considering what amounted essentially to a new government. His motion was defeated, the Articles were scrapped, and the debate on the shape of the new national Congress began. It would last for several months.

The convention deadlocked between the large and small states over the issue of representation. The nationalists in the large-state delegations wanted both houses of the Congress to be based on population, whereas the smaller states wanted equal representation and one vote per state. A further split developed when the South wanted to count their slaves as full human beings while the northern states did not want to count them at all. On June 15, William Paterson of New Jersey offered a plan to counter the Virginia Plan by maintaining state sovereignty and the federal nature of government. The New Jersey Plan preserved the unicameralism, equal representation, and weak executive of the Articles. What Paterson offered was to enlarge the powers of the national Congress over revenue and trade regulations, as well as to make the acts of Congress and treaties the supreme law of the land.

The delegates also made little headway in attempting to create the national executive. Rival ideas about a single or plural executive, a short or long term of office, election by the people, special electors, state legislatures, or the Congress, were all raised with no resolution for weeks on end. All expected Washington to be the first executive, but they could not expect his successors to be as trustworthy with the exercise of power. They struggled to achieve the balance between the tyrannical British king and the ineffectual executives under the Articles. Edmund Randolph feared that a single executive would be the "fetus of monarchy," and fellow Virginian George Mason concurred, asking, "Do gentlemen mean to pave the way to hereditary monarchy?" Pennsylvania's James Wilson answered that, "Unity in the executive . . . would be the best safeguard against tyranny."

The floor of the statehouse was not the only arena where the delegates conversed and politicked. They held informal deliberations at dinners in homes and in taverns. Perhaps many were persuaded on large points and fine ones in this manner, though in early July there was still deadlock. On June 28, Benjamin Franklin called for prayer to restore harmony: "Groping as it was in the dark to find political truth, and scarce able to distinguish it when presented to us, how has it happened, sir, that we have not hitherto once thought of humbly applying to the Father of lights to illuminate our understandings?" Other delegates expressed their despair. Roger Sherman of Connecticut reported that the convention was at a "full stop." Washington lamented having chosen to participate and complained to Alexander Hamilton, who returned to his home in New York, that the councils "are now, if possible, in a worse train than ever . . . I almost *despair* of seeing a favorable issue to the proceedings of the convention." A Fourth of July recess helped soothe tensions and a special committee of eleven was appointed to break the impasse.

On Monday, July 16, the committee's proposals were accepted and became known as the Great Compromise. The House of Representatives would be based upon proportional representation and would originate bills of appropriation. Slaves would count as three-fifths of a person for purposes of calculating representation. The Senate would have an equal vote for all of the states.

On Thursday, July 26, the convention adjourned for several days to allow a Committee of Detail to reconcile and organize all of the resolutions that had been accepted up to that point. On August 6, the committee offered a report that the convention then painstakingly went through line by line for the next month. Meanwhile, the Committee of the Whole and other committees resolved the outstanding contentious points. They created a single president who was to serve for four-year terms. The states would select members of an electoral college (in the same proportion as the Congress) who would elect the president. In addition, a national judiciary was conceived and its jurisdiction established. On September 8, Congress appointed a Committee of Style to draft a constitution, which was largely the work of Gouverneur Morris of Pennsylvania.

Starting September 12, Congress debated the wording of the Constitution for three days. The end of the convention was in sight and the delegates were eager to return home. However, substantive issues were still raised. George Mason argued strenuously for a bill of rights to protect liberties from encroachment and offered to draft it himself in a couple of hours' time. Other opponents argued that the state constitutions already had protections and the convention unanimously rejected Mason's proposal. Mason, Randolph, and Elbridge Gerry then registered their opposition to the document. They wanted the document to go to the state ratifying conventions for revision and then sent back to a second constitutional convention. Other delegates thought this was the best document that could be achieved, even if it was imperfect. Mason resisted calls to sign, averring that he would "sooner chop off his right hand than put it to the Constitution as it now stands."

On September 17, Franklin stated, "I can not help expressing a wish that every member of the Convention who may still have objections to it, would with me, on this occasion doubt a little of his own infallibility, and to make manifest our unanimity, put his name to this instrument." Thirty-nine delegates present from twelve states signed the Constitution. Besides the three opponents who did not sign, the remaining delegates had gone home and were not present. Franklin then pointed to the president's chair which had half a sun on it and mused optimistically: "I have . . . often in the course of the session . . . looked at that behind the President without being able to tell whether it was rising or setting. But now at length I have the happiness to know that it is a rising and not a setting sun." The delegates then repaired to the City Tavern, where they dined with each other and as Washington confided to his diary, "took a cordial leave of each other."

The framers of the Constitution had written a document that embodied the principles of separation of powers, checks and balances, federalism, a limited government with enumerated powers, a written constitution as fundamental law, and popular sovereignty. They had created a *novus ordo seclorum*—a "new order for the ages"—but first the people's representatives in popular ratifying conventions would have to approve it.

· 47 ·

Ratifying Conventions

$\mathcal{O}$n September 19, 1787, the *Pennsylvania Packet* published the Constitution for the people and representatives in Congress and the state legislatures to read. On September 28, Congress voted to send the Constitution as written to the state legislatures so the legislatures could call popular conventions to decide whether to ratify the new framework of government. The supporters of the Constitution would have to win ratification in nine of the thirteen states.

During the debate over ratification, the supporters of the Constitution assumed the mantle of "Federalists" and painted their adversaries as "Anti-Federalists." The Anti-Federalists disputed the title and argued they were defending individual liberty, republican self-government, and the federal principle of balanced power between the national and state governments. They posited that the Constitution would lead to a centralized power in the national government, a republic that was too large, a corrupt senate and judiciary, unlimited taxation, and an aristocracy. Although they were thoughtful and articulate, they were forced to be merely critics rather than defenders of a cohesive alternative plan.

As the respective sides engaged in a war of words in newspapers and pamphlets, the Constitution was experiencing initial successes in the state conventions. By mid-January, 1788, five states—Connecticut, Delaware, Georgia, New Jersey, and Pennsylvania—ratified the Constitution. All these states had only a quick debate on the document and ratified it by a margin more than two to one. Alexander Hamilton and James Madison understood that the main threats would come from the large and important states of Massachusetts, New York, and Virginia, but momentum was building toward ratification.

However, Anti-Federalists were mounting an effective opposition. Most damaging was their critique that the Constitution did not guarantee essential liberties in a bill of rights. They demanded "prior amendments," or changes that would be sent to a second convention before the new government was accepted. During the debate in Massachusetts, the Federalists promised to consider "subsequent" amendments after the Constitution was ratified as written. On February 6, with governor and former Continental Congress president John Hancock supporting ratification, Massachusetts became the sixth state to approve the Constitution by a narrow vote of 187–168.

In New Hampshire, the Federalists thought they did not have the votes to succeed and a week later adjourned the convention until June. Two other states met in the spring, however, and ratified the Constitution, bringing the total to eight. The Federalists in Maryland won by the crushing total of 63–11, and South Carolina became another state to ratify with twice as many votes for the Federalists. Officially, only one more state needed to ratify the Constitution. However, the Constitution might not be considered legitimate if Virginia and New York voted it down. The Federalists believed it essential to win those states.

When the Virginia Convention met on June 2, an enormous struggle took place between many of the giants of the American Revolution. The fiery orator, Patrick Henry, and George Mason fought against ratification with two Federalist masters of political debate, James Madison and John Marshall, and the wavering Edmund Randolph (who had refused to sign the document in Philadelphia) in support. George Washington remained above the ratification fray because of his dislike of partisanship and because he expected to be the first president but his private support was widely known. From Paris, Thomas Jefferson criticized the Constitution for the absence of a bill of rights but favored ratification with prior amendments.

Henry thundered against the Constitution. He warned of the implications of altering "We the states" to "We the people:"

> It was to scrap a confederation and replace it with a great consolidated government, destroying the rights of the states. And other rights, too—

the rights of conscience, liberty of the press, all your communities and franchises, all pretentions to human rights and privileges, are rendered insecure, if not lost, by this change.

Henry continued, warning that the Federalists meant to free all the planters' slaves. The president would lead a standing army to destroy American liberties. "The army will salute him monarch; your militia will fight against you, and what will then become of you and your rights?" he asked. Rather than expressing the genius of the people, as the Federalists claimed, Henry railed, "It is a government by force, and expresses the genius of despotism." Responding to the idea that the government was partly federal, partly national, as Madison averred, Henry mocked, "The brain is national, the stamina federal, this limb national, that limb federal—but what it really signified was that a great consolidated government would be pressing on the necks of the people."

George Mason demanded that the document be examined line by line, and James Madison took that as an opportunity to counter Henry's arguments. When Henry proposed prior amendments as a last ploy, Randolph charged, "The Union will be dissolved, the dogs of war will break loose, and anarchy and discord will complete the ruin of this country," and the idea was defeated. On June 25, the Virginia Convention ratified the Constitution by a vote of eighty-nine to seventy-nine.

Meanwhile, the Anti-Federalists dominated the New York Convention which opened a few weeks after Virginia. Alexander Hamilton defended the Constitution with every fiber of his being and desperately urged his allies in Virginia and New Hampshire to speed word of the outcomes there by express rider to influence the New York debate. The Federalists outmaneuvered the Anti-Federalists by forcing the New York Convention to also scrutinize the Constitution line by line while awaiting news from Virginia and New Hampshire. Hamilton's couriers brought the news that both those states had ratified the Constitution to make it the fundamental law of the land. Bells pealed and cannons were fired to celebrate, but the struggle at Poughkeepsie continued. In the middle of the debate, Hamilton wondered if he should permit prior amendments. Madison admonished his friend that "a conditional ratification . . . was itself considered as worse than a rejection." On July 26, New York finally did ratify the Constitution by the slimmest of margins: 30–27. North Carolina and Rhode Island would follow in time.

The American people ratified the new framework of government to protect the liberties they had fought for and won in the American Revolution. The deliberations about the principles of republican government defined not only the American government but the American character.

· 48 ·

The Federalist

$\mathcal{A}$fter the Constitution was published and sent to the states for ratification, the opponents of the new Constitution rallied quickly and penned essays against it. Its supporters were alarmed by the force of these arguments. Alexander Hamilton noted that, "The artillery of its opponents makes some impression." James Madison worried that "the newspapers here begin to teem with vehement and virulent calumniations of the proposed government."

In mid-October, Hamilton was traveling from Albany, where he was attending the session of the New York Supreme Court, to his home in New York City. During his leisure time sailing on the Hudson by sloop, he outlined a plan to write a number of essays in defense of the Constitution against its critics. He sought to demonstrate that the national government would have the vigor to act while not endangering the liberties of the people. He enlisted the help of the ardent nationalist and "father of the Constitution," James Madison, as well as New York diplomat and president of the Continental Congress, John Jay. Gouverneur Morris declined to make any contributions when asked, and William Duer's submission was awful enough not to include. Jay fell ill after working on essays #2 through #5 and had to back out of the project. It was left to Hamilton and Madison to write the essays.

The first *Federalist*, as the essays were called, appeared in the New York *Independent Journal* on October 27. Hamilton addressed his essay to the "people of the State of New York," but his true audience was the delegates to the New York Ratifying Convention, where opposition was strong. Though *The Federalist* would come to be seen as much more, it was written as propaganda and aimed at the Anti-Federalists, especially at the New York convention. It was published in four of New York City's five newspapers.

The Federalist was written at the frenetic pace of nearly 1,000 words per day. There were usually two entries in each newspaper edition, overwhelming the opposition, the printers, and the authors. Hamilton and Madison were able to accomplish their Herculean writing task because of their extensive knowledge of ancient and modern history and political philosophy, partly as a result of their preparation for and experience at the Annapolis and Philadelphia Conventions. They conferred on the early entries. As Madison wrote, "In the beginning it was the practice of the writers . . . to communicate each to the other, their respective papers before they were sent to the press." They wrote as Publius, the Roman ruler who nobly countered the suspicions that he sought to usurp the people.

When *Federalist* #1 appeared on October 27, Hamilton laid down the importance of the deliberations about their Constitution. He wrote:

> It seems to have been reserved to the people of this country, by their conduct and example, to decide the important question, whether societies of men are really capable or not of establishing good government from reflection and choice, or whether they are forever destined to depend upon their political constitutions on accident and force.

By January 11, 1788, Madison agreed to write the next twenty-two essays beginning with *Federalist* #37. Hamilton took a break to attend to his legal practice. To assuage Anti-Federalist fears of a national leviathan that would destroy the states, Madison explained in *Federalist* #39 that the plan of government was "neither a national nor a federal Constitution, but a composition of both." Hamilton soon re-entered the fray and penned the rest of the essays while Madison went home to Virginia to fight for ratification.

By early February, six states had ratified the Constitution including the critically important Massachusetts, but New York and Virginia still had not met. Therefore, Hamilton and Madison published the *Federalist* in book form on March 22, rearranging the order of the essays for logical sequence. The first thirty-six essays were nicely bound in a format that could be easily distributed to the delegates of the New York Convention and around the country.

By April 2, the last of the *Federalist* essays—number seventy-seven—was published in newspapers. On May 28, just weeks before the New York and Virginia conventions were scheduled to convene, the second volume of *The Federalist* was published in book form. Hamilton had written an additional eight essays for the book that never appeared in the newspapers. Among their number was *Federalist #78* in which he called the judiciary "the least dangerous" branch and argued for its power to "declare all acts contrary to the manifest tenor of the Constitution void." In Federalist #84, Hamilton answered the important Anti-Federalist objection that the Constitution lacked a bill of rights. Hamilton contended that the written constitution granted the limited, republican national government enumerated powers and it had no authority to violate the rights of the sovereign people in the first place. In the next and last essay, he imputed the motives of his opponents, warning of the dismal price of failure: "I dread the more the consequences of new attempts because I know the POWERFUL INDIVIDUALS, in this [New York] and in other states, are enemies to a general national government in every possible shape."

The Federalist shaped the debate over the ratification of the Constitution. It was a brilliant piece of political propaganda, Yet many contemporary observers noted its importance to republican political theory. George Washington described it as throwing "new light upon the science of government [and] they have given the rights of man a full and fair discussion." Future Supreme Court chief justice John Marshall thought that it "will be read and admired when the controversy in which that valuable treatise on government originated, shall no longer be remembered." Thomas Jefferson praised *The Federalist* simply as "the best commentary on the principles of government which ever was written."

· 49 ·

Inauguration of George Washington

$\mathcal{W}$ith eleven states having ratified the Constitution, the new government was scheduled to go into operation in the spring of 1789. In September 1788, Congress had directed the states to choose presidential electors. On February 4, the electors met to select the president and vice president of the United States. Unsurprisingly, they unanimously selected George Washington to be the nation's first president. John Adams, who came in a distant second, thus became the vice president, as provided for in the Constitution.

Washington was chosen president for his character and republican virtue. He was the disinterested Cincinnatus who had served his country during the American Revolution and voluntarily surrendered that power. He reluctantly came out of retirement to serve as president of the Constitutional Convention and supported its ratification. His fellow Americans expected the "indispensable man" to serve as the new nation's first executive. Indeed, the office of the presidency was created with Washington in mind, because he could be trusted with power.

Washington struggled with the decision to accept the presidency and sought the advice of several confidants. He feared the world would accuse him of "*inconsistency* and *ambition*" because of his former promise to retire permanently to his "vine and fig tree." He told Marquis de Lafayette that he was facing the office with "unfeigned reluctance" and that "nothing short of a conviction of duty will induce me again to take an active part in public affairs." But, Washington understood his own importance to the success of the new government. He wished to know from Alexander Hamilton "whether there does not exist a probability that the government would be just as happily and effectually carried into execution without my aid, as with it." Hamilton advised that Washington had no choice but to answer the "general call of your country in relation to the new government." He reluctantly accepted, determined to lend "whatever assistance might be in my power to promote the public weal, in hopes that at a convenient and early period . . . I might be permitted once more to retire."

Washington might have wished for a quiet journey to New York, the capital of the new nation, for his inauguration, but tens of thousands of his fellow citizens celebrated their general along the way in Alexandria, Baltimore, Wilmington, Philadelphia, Trenton, and Princeton. They held grand dinners and parties, made toasts, recited odes, threw flowers, fired cannons, and offered honor escorts. Washington told his friend Henry Knox that becoming president was "accompanied with feelings not unlike those of a culprit who is going to the place of execution."

On April 30, Washington, dressed in a suit of fine black velvet, white silk stockings, and silver buckles, stood on an open portico of Federal Hall before a throng assembled on Wall Street. Robert Livingston, chancellor of New York, administered the oath of office. When Washington finished, he may have stated "so help me God" and reached down and kissed the Bible. (There is some debate over whether this happened.) Livingston proclaimed, "Long live George Washington, the President of the United States!" The crowd roared its approval and church bells pealed throughout the city.

A grave and stiff Washington then delivered his First Inaugural Address to the Congress. Like all of his speeches, he began deferentially, claiming to be a disinterested republican statesman who wished to be on his plantation but was "summoned by my country." He humbly thanked God for the providential blessings on the American people and their experiment with republican liberty. "The preservation of the sacred fire of liberty, and the destiny of the republican model of government, are justly considered as deeply, perhaps as finally, staked on the experiment entrusted to the hands of the American people." Washington hoped that Americans would be united by the national Union, not "local prejudices or attachments—no separate views, nor party animosities." He encouraged Congress to pass a Bill of Rights for the sake of national harmony. He predicted success if republican ideals remained at the core of the

American character: "The foundations of our national policy will be laid in the pure and immutable principles of private morality, and the preeminence of free government be exemplified by all the attributes which can win the affections of its citizens, and command the respect of the world." For the next week, President Washington and each house of Congress exchanged gushing messages of mutual admiration.

The Congress then debated titles for the president for nearly three weeks. Vice President Adams wanted to establish a high tone and dignity for the office with titles like "His Highness, the President of the United States of America, and Protector of their Liberties." Adams's opponents felt that titles like these sounded as though they belonged in a monarchy, not a republic. Some mocked Adams and the whole debate, one person calling him "His Rotundity." Congress finally settled on the simple republican "President of the United States." Washington chose talented officials such as Alexander Hamilton, Thomas Jefferson, Henry Knox, and Edmund Randolph to help him run the executive branch, even though a cabinet was not strictly provided for in the Constitution. Washington set numerous precedents, acted with the dignity all expected, promoted Union, and helped to establish a vigorous constitutional republic at home and among the great powers. Perhaps most important, he established a legacy of surrendering power once again when he resigned from office after two terms.

· 50 ·

Bill of Rights

*A*lthough a bill of rights was unanimously rejected toward the end of the Constitutional Convention, the Federalists had been forced to promise one to win ratification in Massachusetts, Virginia, and New York. James Madison sought to fulfill that promise in the First Congress.

Hoping to win support in Congress for a second convention and to weaken the power of the national government, Virginia governor Patrick Henry used his influence in the Virginia Assembly to block Madison's election to the senate. Madison instead ran for a seat in the House of Representatives. During this election, Madison publicly supported amendments to the Constitution to protect individual liberties. As he admitted privately to Thomas Jefferson, he did not think a bill of rights absolutely necessary but agreed that "it might be of use, and if properly executed could not be of disservice." He believed that a bill of rights might prove to be merely a "parchment barrier" that could be ignored by a tyrannical majority. But, he recognized that the "friends of the Constitution, some from an approbation of particular amendments, others from a spirit of conciliation, are generally agreed that the system should be revised." He concurred, as long as "the revisal to be carried no farther than to supply additional guards for liberty, without abridging the sum of power transferred from the states to the general government." It was also essential that Congress deliver a bill of rights rather than a second convention dominated by committed Anti-Federalists.

In his First Inaugural Address, President George Washington lent his considerable prestige to the effort when he encouraged legislators in Congress to pass a bill of rights for the states to consider. He advised them to avoid tampering with the powers of the national government, but hoped "a reverence for the characteristic rights of freemen, and a regard for the public harmony, will sufficiently influence your deliberations on the question."

On June 8, the House took up the measure. Madison stated that he wished to prove that the Federalists "were as sincerely devoted to liberty and a republican government" as their opponents. "It was a desirable thing," he asserted, "to extinguish from the bosom of every member of the community any apprehensions, that there are those among his countrymen who wish to deprive them of the liberty for which they valiantly fought and honorably bled." Besides winning over the Anti-Federalists, the American people, and the hold-out states of Rhode Island and North Carolina, the most important advantage of a bill of rights was "the abuse of the powers of the general government may be guarded against in a more secure manner than is now done."

Members of Congress opposed amendments for a variety of reasons. Henry's allies continued to press for another convention. Federalists contended that Congress had more pressing business and could not be bogged down in a debate over amendments. Moreover, they still argued that a bill of rights was unnecessary to protect individual liberties since the Constitution did not empower the national government to violate them.

Madison failed to get all he wanted. He wanted the bill of rights to be placed into the body of the Constitution rather than as amendments at the end of the document. He wanted a provision to prohibit the states from interfering with rights of conscience, a free press, and jury trials, but the Senate roundly defeated it. The Bill of Rights would apply only to the federal government, a principle later reaffirmed by the Supreme Court in *Barron v. Baltimore* (1833).

The House delivered seventeen amendments to the Senate by August 24. On September 14, the Senate agreed to twelve amendments, and conference committees reconciled the differences. By September 25, both houses of Congress had voted for twelve amendments and President Washington duly sent them to the states for ratification. The states ratified ten of the twelve amendments (one of the proposed amendments that failed—preventing Congress from voting itself a pay raise—would later be ratified in 1992 as the Twenty-seventh Amendment).

The Bill of Rights protected essential liberties of the American people—freedom of speech, freedom of religion, the right to bear arms, and a trial by jury. It also limited the national government's ability to search homes and persons, take private property, and punish those convicted of crimes excessively. Finally, it reserved to the people and the states all other rights, including those that were not listed.

The Bill of Rights persuaded North Carolina and Rhode Island to ratify the Constitution, bringing them into the Union. By December 15, 1791, Virginia ratified the amendments. The ten Amendments known as the Bill of Rights included such fundamental American principles as freedom of religion and freedom of speech and the right to a trial by jury. They became enshrined as the fundamental law of the land. Though the meaning of these amendments has been debated throughout America's history, Madison was undeniably correct in stating: "The political truths declared in that solemn manner acquire by degrees the character of fundamental maxims of free government."

Bibliography

GENERAL COLONIAL AMERICA

Boorstin, Daniel J. *The Americans: The Colonial Experience.* New York: Vintage, 1958.

Fischer, David Hackett. *Albion's Seed: Four British Folkways in America.* Oxford: Oxford University Press, 1989.

Hawke, David Freeman. *Everyday Life in Early America.* New York: Harper and Row, 1988.

Risjord, Norman K. *The Colonists: Representative Americans.* 2nd ed. Lanham, MD: Rowman & Littlefield, 2001.

Taylor, Alan. *American Colonies: The Settling of North America.* New York: Penguin, 2001.

LOST COLONY

Horn, James. *A Kingdom Strange: The Brief and Tragic History of the Lost Colony of Roanoke.* New York: Basic Books, 2010.

Kupperman, Karen O. *Roanoke: The Abandoned Colony.* 2nd ed. Lanham, MD: Rowman & Littlefield, 2007.

Miller, Lee. *Roanoke: Solving the Mystery of the Lost Colony.* New York: Penguin, 2000.

Quinn, David Beers. *Set Fair for Roanoke: Voyages and Colonies, 1584–1606.* Chapel Hill: University of North Carolina Press, 1985.

JAMESTOWN COLONY, STARVING TIME, FIRST REPRESENTATIVE LEGISLATURE

Deans, Bob. *The River Where America Began: A Journey Along the James.* Lanham, MD: Rowman & Littlefield, 2007.

Doherty, Kieran. *Sea Venture: Shipwreck, Survival, and the Salvation of the First English Colony in the New World*. New York: St. Martin's Press, 2007.

Glover, Lorri and Daniel Blake Smith. *The Shipwreck that Saved Jamestown: The Sea Venture Castaways and the Fate of America*. New York: Henry Holt, 2008.

Hoobler, Thomas and Dorothy Hoobler. *Captain John Smith: Jamestown and the Birth of the American Dream*. Hoboken, NJ: John Wiley and Sons, 2006.

Horn, James. *A Land As God Made It: Jamestown and the Birth of America*. New York: Basic, 2005.

Kelso, William M. *Jamestown: The Buried Truth*. Charlottesville: University of Virginia Press, 2006.

Kupperman, Karen Ordahl. *The Jamestown Project*. Cambridge, MA: Harvard University Press, 2007.

Price, David A. *Love and Hate in Jamestown: John Smith, Pocahontas, and the Heart of a New Nation*. New York: Knopf, 2003.

Tate, Thad W. and David L. Ammerman, eds. *The Chesapeake in the Seventeenth Century: Essays on Anglo-American Society*. New York: Norton, 1979.

Vaughan, Alden T. *American Genesis: Captain John Smith and the Founding of Virginia*. Boston: Little, Brown, 1975.

FIRST AFRICANS

Hashaw, Tim. *The Birth of Black America: The First African Americans and the Pursuit of Freedom at Jamestown*. New York: Carroll & Graf, 2007.

Jordan, Winthrop D. *White over Black: American Attitudes Toward the Negro, 1550–1812*. New York: Norton, 1968.

Morgan, Edmund S. *American Slavery, American Freedom: The Ordeal of Colonial Virginia*. New York: Norton, 1975.

Wood, Betty. *The Origins of American Slavery: Freedom and Bondage in the English Colonies*. New York: Hill and Wang, 1997.

Wright, Donald R. *African Americans in the Colonial Era: From African Origins Through the American Revolution*. Arlington Heights, IL: Harlan Davidson, 1990.

MAYFLOWER COMPACT, CITY UPON A HILL

Bradford, William. *Of Plymouth Plantation*. Mineola, NY: Dover, 2006.

Bremer, Francis J. *John Winthrop: America's Forgotten Founding Father*. New York: Oxford University Press, 2003.

Miller, Perry. *Errand into the Wilderness*. New York: Harper and Row, 1956.

Morgan, Edmund S. *The Puritan Dilemma: The Story of John Winthrop.* Boston: Little, Brown, 1958.

Philbrick, Nathaniel. *Mayflower: A Story of Courage, Community, and War.* New York: Viking, 2006.

Warner, Michael, ed. *American Sermons: The Pilgrims to Martin Luther King, Jr.* New York: Library of Freedom, 1999.

Witham, Larry. *A City Upon a Hill: How Sermons Changed the Course of American History.* New York: Harper Collins, 2007.

INDIAN UPRISING OF 1622

Kupperman, Karen Ordahl. *Indians and English: Facing Off in Early America.* Ithaca: Cornell University Press, 2000.

Rountree, Helen C. *Pocahontas, Powhatan, Opechancanough: Three Indian Lives Changed by Jamestown.* Charlottesville: University of Virginia Press, 2005.

———. *The Powhatan Indians: Their Traditional Culture.* Norman: University of Oklahoma Press, 1989.

DISSENTS OF ANNE HUTCHINSON AND ROGER WILLIAMS

LaPlante, Eve. *American Jezebel: The Uncommon Life of Anne Hutchinson, The Woman who Defied the Puritans.* New York: Harper Collins, 2004.

Miller, Perry. *Roger Williams: His Contribution to the American Tradition.* New York: Antheneum, 1970.

Morgan, Edmund S. *Roger Williams: The Church and the State.* New York: Harcourt, Brace, 1967.

PEQUOT WAR

Cave, Alfred A. *The Pequot War.* Amherst: University of Massachusetts Press, 1996.

Katz, Steven T. "The Pequot War Reconsidered." In Alden T. Vaughan, ed. *New England Encounters: Indians and Euroamericans, ca. 1600–1850.* Boston: Northeastern University Press, 1999.

Salisbury, Neal. *Manuitou and Providence: Indians, Europeans, and the Making of New England, 1500–1643.* New York: Oxford University Press, 1982.

Steele, Ian K. *Warpaths: Invasions of North America.* New York: Oxford University Press, 1994.

KING PHILIP'S WAR

Lepore, Jill. *The Name of War: King Philip's War and the Origins of American Identity.* New York: New York: Vintage, 1998.

Leach, Douglas Edward. *Flintlock and Tomahawk: New England in King Philip's War.* Woodstock, VT: The Countryman Press, 2009. Orig. pub. 1958.

Schultz, Eric B. and Michael J. Tougias. *King Philip's War: The History and Legacy of America's Forgotten Conflict.* Woodstock, VT: The Countryman Press, 1999.

BACON'S REBELLION

Craven, Welsey Frank. *The Southern Colonies in the Seventeenth Century, 1607–1689.* Baton Rouge: Louisiana State University Press, 1949.

Washburn, Wilcomb E. *The Governor and the Rebel: A History of Bacon's Rebellion in Virginia.* Chapel Hill: University of North Carolina Press, 1957.

Webb, Stephen Saunders. *1676: The End of American Independence.* Cambridge: Harvard University Press, 1985.

GLORIOUS REVOLUTION IN AMERICA

Breen, T. H. *The Character of the Good Ruler: Puritan Political Ideas in New England, 1630–1730.* New York: Norton, 1970.

Hall, Michael G. *The Last American Puritan: The Life of Increase Mather.* Hanover, NH: University Press of New England, 1988.

Lovejoy, David S. *The Glorious Revolution in America.* New York: Harper and Row, 1972.

SALEM WITCH TRIALS

Boyer, Paul, and Stephen Nissenbaum. *Salem Possessed: The Social Origins of Witchcraft.* Cambridge, MA: Harvard University Press, 1974.

Hill, Frances. *A Delusion of Satan: The Full Story of the Salem Witch Trials.* Cambridge, MA: Da Capo, 2002.

Karlsen, Carol F. *The Devil in the Shape of a Woman: Witchcraft in Colonial New England.* New York: Vintage, 1987.

LaPlante, Eve. *Salem Witch Judge: The Life and Repentance of Samuel Sewall.* New York: Harper Collins, 2007.

Norton, Mary Beth. *In the Devil's Snare: The Salem Witchcraft Trials of 1692.* New York: Vintage, 2002.

Silverman, Kenneth. *The Life and Times of Cotton Mather.* New York: Columbia University Press, 1985.

Starkey, Marion L. *The Devil in Massachusetts: A Modern Enquiry into the Salem Witch Trials.* New York: Alfred A. Knopf, 1949.

BOSTON SMALLPOX EPIDEMIC OF 1721

Blake, John B. "The Inoculation Controversy in Boston: 1721–1722." *New England Quarterly* 25 (December 1952): 489–506.

Hopkins, Donald R. *The Greatest Killer: Smallpox in History.* Chicago: University of Chicago Press, 1983.

Minardi, Margot. "The Boston Inoculation Controversy of 1721–1722: An Incident in the History of Race." *William and Mary Quarterly,* 3rd ser., 61 (January, 2004): 47–76.

Van de Wetering, Maxine. "A Reconsideration of the Inoculation Controversy." *New England Quaterly* 58 (March 1985): 46–67.

Williams, Tony. *The Pox and the Covenant: Mather, Franklin, and the Epidemic that Changed America's Destiny.* Naperville, IL: Sourcebooks, 2010.

Winslow, Ola Elizabeth. *A Destroying Angel: The Conquest of Smallpox in Colonial Boston.* Boston: Houghton, Mifflin, 1974.

GREAT AWAKENING

Bonomi, Patricia U. *Under the Cope of Heaven: Religion, Society, and Politics in Colonial America.* New York: Oxford University Press, 1986.

Butler, Jon. *Awash in a Sea of Faith: Christianizing the American People.* Cambridge, MA: Harvard University Press, 1990.

Isaac, Rhys. *The Transformation of Virginia, 1740–1790.* New York: Norton, 1982.

Stout, Harry S. *The New England Soul: Preaching and Religious Culture in Colonial New England.* New York: Oxford University Press, 1986.

BENJAMIN FRANKLIN AND THE LIGHTNING ROD

Chaplin, Joyce E. *The First Scientist: Benjamin Franklin and the Pursuit of Genius.* New York: Basic Books, 2006.

Cohen, I. Bernard. *Benjamin Franklin's Science*. Cambridge: Harvard University Press, 1990.

Dray, Philip. *Stealing God's Thunder: Benjamin Franklin's Lightning Rod and the Invention of America*. New York: Random House, 2005.

Isaacson, Walter. *Benjamin Franklin: An American Life*. New York: Simon & Schuster, 2003.

Krider, E. Philip. "Benjamin Franklin's Science." In *Benjamin Franklin: In Search of a Better World*. Edited by Page Talbott. New Haven: Yale University Press, 2005.

Morgan, Edmund S. *Benjamin Franklin*. New Haven: Yale University Press, 2002.

Van Doren, Carl. *Benjamin Franklin*. New York: Penguin, 1938.

Wood, Gordon S. *The Americanization of Benjamin Franklin*. New York: Penguin, 2004.

ALBANY PLAN OF UNION, ROYAL PROCLAMATION OF 1763

Anderson, Fred. *Crucible of War: The Seven Years' War and the Fate of Empire in British North America, 1754–1766*. New York: Vintage, 2000.

Axelrod, Alan. *Blooding at Great Meadows: Young George Washington and the Battle that Shaped the Man*. Philadelphia: Running Press, 2007.

Borneman, Walter R. *The French and Indian War: Deciding the Fate of North America*. New York: Harper, 2006.

Calloway, Colin G. *The Scratch of a Pen: 1763 and the Transformation of North America*. Oxford: Oxford University Press, 2006.

Holton, Woody. *Forced Founders: Indians, Debtors, Slaves, and the Making of the American Revolution in Virginia*. Chapel Hill: University of North Carolina Press, 1999.

GENERAL PRIMARY SOURCES ON THE AMERICAN REVOLUTION

Commager, Henry Steele and Richard B. Morris, eds. *The Spirit of 'Seventy-Six: The Story of the American Revolution as Told by Participants*. New York: De Capo, 1995.

Rhodehamel, John, ed. *The American Revolution: Writings from the War of Independence*. New York: Library of America, 2001.

Spalding, Matthew, ed. *The Founders' Almanac: A Practical Guide to the Notable Events, Greatest Leaders, and Most Eloquent Words of the American Founding*. Washington, DC: Heritage Foundation, 2001.

GENERAL BOOKS ON THE
AMERICAN REVOLUTION

Bailyn, Bernard. *The Ideological Origins of the American Revolution*. Cambridge: Harvard University Press, 1967.

Ellis, Joseph J. *American Creation: Triumphs and Tragedies at the Founding of the Republic*. New York: Knopf, 2007.

Ferling, John. *Almost a Miracle: The American Victory in the War of Independence*. Oxford: Oxford University Press, 2007.

———. *A Leap in the Dark: The Struggle to Create the American Republic*. Oxford: Oxford University Press, 2003.

Higginbotham, Don. *The War of American Independence: Military Attitudes, Policies, and Practice, 1763–1789*. Boston: Northeastern University Press, 1971.

Middlekauff, Robert. *The Glorious Cause: The American Revolution, 1763–1789*. Oxford: Oxford University Press, 1982.

Morgan, Edmund S. *The Birth of the Republic, 1763–1789*. Chicago: University of Chicago Press, 1956.

Rakove, Jack. *Revolutionaries: A New History of the Invention of America*. Boston: Houghton Mifflin Harcourt, 2010.

Wood, Gordon. *The American Revolution*. New York: Modern Library, 2003.

———. *The Creation of the American Republic, 1776–1787*. New York: Norton, 1969.

———. *The Radicalism of the American Revolution*. New York: Vintage, 1991.

STAMP ACT, TOWNSHEND ACTS

Beeman, Richard R. *Patrick Henry: A Biography*. New York: McGraw-Hill, 1974.

Maier, Pauline. *From Resistance to Revolution: Colonial Radicals and the Development of American Opposition to Britain, 1765–1776*. New York: Norton, 1972.

Meade, Robert Douthat. *Patrick Henry: Patriot in the Making*. Philadelphia: J. B. Lippincott, 1957.

Morgan, Edmund S. and Helen M. Morgan. *The Stamp Act Crisis: Prologue to Revolution*. Chapel Hill: University of North Carolina Press, 1953.

BOSTON MASSACRE

Archer, Richard. *As If an Enemy's Country: The British Occupation of Boston and the Origins of Revolution*. Oxford: Oxford University Press, 2010.

Zobel, Hiller B. *The Boston Massacre*. New York: Norton, 1970.

BOSTON TEA PARTY

Young, Alfred F. *The Shoemaker and the Tea Party.* Boston: Beacon Press, 1999.

CONTINENTAL CONGRESS

Labaree, Benjamin Woods. *The Boston Tea Party.* Boston: Northeastern University Press, 1979.

Rakove, Jack. *The Beginnings of National Politics: An Interpretive History of the Continental Congress.* New York: Alfred A. Knopf, 1979.

LEXINGTON AND CONCORD

Fischer, David Hackett. *Paul Revere's Ride.* New York: Oxford University Press, 1994.

Gross, Robert A. *The Minutemen and Their World.* New York: Hill and Wang, 1976.

BUNKER HILL

Ketchum, Richard M. *Decisive Day: The Battle for Bunker Hill.* New York: Henry Holt, 1962.

FORT TICONDEROGA

McCullough, David. *1776.* New York: Simon and Schuster, 2005.

Puls, Mark. *Henry Knox: Visionary General of the American Revolution.* New York: Palgrave Macmillan, 2008.

COMMON SENSE

Foner, Eric. *Tom Paine and Revolutionary America.* London: Oxford University Press, 1976.

Liell, Scott. *46 Pages: Thomas Paine,* Common Sense, *and the Turning Point to Independence.* Philadelphia: Running Press, 2003.

Paine, Thomas. Rights of Man, Common Sense, *and Other Political Writing*. Mark Philip, ed. Oxford: Oxford University Press, 1995.

DECLARATION OF RIGHTS

Broadwater, Jeff. *George Mason: Forgotten Founder.* Chapel Hill: University of North Carolina Press, 2006.

Davis, Burke. *A Williamsburg Galaxy.* Williamsburg, VA: Colonial Williamsburg Foundation, 1968.

Rutland, Robert. *George Mason: Reluctant Statesman.* Charlottesville: University of Virginia Press, 1961.

Selby, John E. *The Revolution in Virginia.* Williamsburg, VA: Colonial Williamsburg Foundation, 1988.

DECLARATION OF INDEPENDENCE

Becker, Carl. *The Declaration of Independence: A Study in the History of Political Ideas.* New York: Vintage, 1922.

Declaration of Independence (Various editions)

Hogeland, William. *Declaration: The Nine Tumultuous Weeks When America Became Independent, May 1–July4, 1776.* New York: Simon & Schuster, 2010.

Maier, Pauline. *American Scripture: Making the Declaration of Independence.* New York: Vintage, 1997.

Wills, Garry. *Inventing America: Jefferson's Declaration of Independence.* Garden City, NY: Doubleday, 1978.

CROSSING THE DELAWARE

Fischer, David Hackett. *Washington's Crossing.* Oxford: Oxford University Press, 2004.

Ketchum, Richard M. *The Winter Soldiers: The Battles for Trenton and Princeton.* New York: Henry Holt, 1973.

McCullough, David. *1776.* New York: Simon and Schuster, 2005.

SARATOGA

Ketchum, Richard M. *Saratoga: Turning Point of America's Revolutionary War.* New York: Henry Holt, 1997.

FRENCH ALLIANCE, PEACE TREATY OF 1783

Bemis, Samuel Flagg. *The Diplomacy of the American Revolution*. Bloomington: Indiana University Press, 1935.

Dull, Jonathan R. *A Diplomatic History of the American Revolution*. New Haven: Yale University Press, 1985.

Fleming, Thomas. *The Perils of Peace: America's Struggle for Survival after Yorktown*. New York: Smithsonian Books, 2007.

Morris, Richard B. *The Peacemakers: The Great Powers and American Independence*. New York: Harper and Row, 1965.

Paul, Joel Richard. *Unlikely Allies: How a Merchant, a Playwright, and a Spy Saved the American Revolution*. New York: Riverhead Books, 2009.

Stinchcombe, William C. *The American Revolution and the French Alliance*. Syracuse: Syracuse University Press, 1969.

VALLEY FORGE

Fleming, Thomas. *Washington's Secret War: The Hidden History of Valley Forge*. New York: Smithsonian Books, 2005.

Lockhart, Paul. *The Drillmaster of Valley Forge: The Baron De Steuben and the Making of an American Army*. New York: Smithsonian Books, 2008.

GUILFORD COURTHOUSE

Babits, Lawrence E. and Joshua B. Howard. *Long, Obstinate, and Bloody: The Battle of Guilford Courthouse*. Chapel Hill: University of North Carolina Press, 2009.

Carbonne, Gerald M. *Nathanael Greene: A Biography of the American Revolution*. New York: Palgrave Macmillan, 2008.

Golway, Terry. *Washington's General: Nathaniel Greene and the Triumph of the American Revolution*. New York: Henry Holt, 2006.

YORKTOWN

Ketchum, Richard M. *Victory at Yorktown: The Campaign that Won the Revolution*. New York: Henry Holt, 2004.

NEWBURGH CONSPIRACY, WASHINGTON SURRENDERS HIS COMMISSION

Brookhiser, Richard. *Founding Father: Rediscovering George Washington.* New York: Free Press, 1996.

Ellis, Joseph J. *His Excellency: George Washington.* New York: Knopf, 2004.

Higginbotham, Don. *George Washington: United a Nation.* Lanham, MD: Rowman & Littlefield, 2002.

Kohn, Richard H. *Eagle and Sword: The Beginnings of the Military Establishment in America.* New York: Free Press, 1975.

Weintraub, Stanley. *General Washington's Christmas Farewell: A Mount Vernon Homecoming, 1783.* New York: Free Press, 2003.

Wills, Garry. *Cincinnatus: George Washington and the Enlightenment: Images of Power in Early America.* New York: Doubleday, 1984.

VIRGINIA STATUTE FOR RELIGIOUS FREEDOM

Dreisbach, Daniel L., Mark D. Hall, and Jeffry H. Morrison, eds. *The Founders on God and Government.* Lanham, MD: Rowman & Littlefield, 2004.

Hutson, James H. *Religion and the Founding of the American Republic.* Washington, DC: Library of Congress, 1998.

Hutson, James H., ed. *Religion and the New Republic: Faith in the Founding of America.* Lanham, MD: Rowman & Littlefield, 2000.

Miller, William Lee. *The First Liberty: America's Foundation in Religious Freedom.* Rev. ed. Washington, DC: Georgetown University Press, 2003.

Palm. Daniel C., ed. *On Faith and Free Government.* Lanham, MD: Rowman & Littlefield, 1997.

Waldman, Steven. *Founding Faith: Providence, Politics, and the Birth of Religious Freedom in America.* New York: Random House, 2008.

SHAYS' REBELLION

Richards, Leonard L. *Shays' Rebellion: The American Revolution's Final Battle.* Philadelphia: University of Pennsylvania Press, 2002.

Szatmary, David P. *Shays' Rebellion: The Making of an Agrarian Insurrection.* Amherst: The University of Massachusetts Press, 1980.

ANNAPOLIS CONVENTION, CONSTITUTIONAL CONVENTION

Beeman, Richard. *Plain, Honest Men: The Making of the American Constitution.* New York: Random House, 2009.

Berkin, Carol. *A Brilliant Solution: Inventing the American Constitution.* New York: Harcourt, 2002.

Bowen, Catherine Drinker. *Miracle at Philadelphia: The Story of the Constitutional Convention May to September 1787.* Boston: Little Brown, 1966.

Farrand, Max. *The Framing of the Constitution of the United States.* New Haven: Yale University Press, 1913.

Ketcham, Ralph. *Framed for Posterity: The Enduring Philosophy of the Constitution.* Lawrence, KS: University Press of Kansas, 1993.

McDonald, Forrest. *Novus Ordo Seclorum: The Intellectual Origins of the Constitution.* Lawrence: University Press of Kansas, 1985.

Stewart, David O. *The Summer of 1787: The Men Who Invented the Constitution.* New York: Simon & Schuster, 2007.

Van Doren, Carl. *The Great Rehearsal. The Story of the Making and Ratifying of the Constitution of the United States.* New York: Time, Inc.: 1965.

RATIFYING CONVENTIONS, THE FEDERALIST

Allen, W. B. and Gordon Lloyd, eds. *The Essential Anti-Federalist.* Lanham, MD: Rowman & Littlefield, 2002.

Bailyn, Bernard, ed. *The Debate on the Constitution: Federalist and Anti-Federalist Speeches, Articles, and Letters During the Struggle over Ratification.* 2 vols. New York: Library of America, 1993.

Chadwick, Bruce. *Triumvirate: The Story of the Unlikely Alliance that Saved the Constitution and United the Nation.* Naperville, IL: Sourcebooks, 2009.

Cornell, Saul. *The Other Founders: Anti-Federalism and the Dissenting Tradition in America, 1788–1828.* Chapel Hill: University of North Carolina Press, 1999.

Ketcham, Ralph, ed. *The Anti-Federalist Papers and the Constitutional Convention Debates.* New York: New American Library, 1986.

Main, Jackson Turner. *The Anti-Federalists: Critics of the Constitution, 1781–1788.* Chapel Hill: University of North Carolina Press, 1961.

Meyerson, Michael I. *Liberty's Blueprint: How Madison and Hamilton Wrote the Federalist Papers, Defined the Constitution, and Made Democracy Safe for the World.* New York: Basic, 2008.

Morris, Richard B. *Witnesses at the Creation: Hamilton, Madison, Jay, and the Constitution*. New York: Holt, Rinehart, and Winston, 1985.

Rakove, Jack. *Original Meanings: Politics and Ideas in the Making of the Constitution*. New York: Vintage, 1996.

Storing, Herbert. *What the Anti-Federalists were for: The Political Thought of the Opponents of the Constitution*. Chicago: University of Chicago Press, 1981.

Wills, Garry. *Explaining America: The Federalist*. Garden City, New York: Doubleday, 1981.

INAUGURATION OF GEORGE WASHINGTON

Allen, W. B., ed. *George Washington: A Collection*. Indianapolis, IN: Liberty Fund, 1988.

McDonald, Forrest. *The Presidency of George Washington*. Lawrence: University of Kansas Press, 1974.

Smith, Richard Norton. *Patriarch: George Washington and the New Nation*. Boston: Houghton Mifflin, 1993.

Wood, Gordon. *Empire of Liberty: A History of the Early Republic, 1789–1815*. Oxford: Oxford University Press, 2009.

BILL OF RIGHTS

Elkins, Stanley and Eric McKitrick. *The Age of Federalism: The Early American Republic, 1788–1800*. New York: Oxford University Press, 1993.

Labunski, Richard. *James Madison and the Struggle for the Bill of Rights*. Oxford: Oxford University Press, 2006.

Lloyd, Gordon and Margie Lloyd, eds. *The Essential Bill of Rights: Original Arguments and Fundamental Documents*. Lanham, MD: University Press of America, 1998.

Rutland, Robert Allen. *The Birth of the Bill of Rights, 1776–1791*. Rev. ed. Boston: Northeastern University Press, 1983.

Veit, Helen E., Kenneth R. Bowling, and Charlene Bangs Bickford, eds. *Creating the Bill of Rights: The Documentary Record from the First Congress*. Baltimore: The Johns Hopkins University Press 1991.

Index